THE TIMES TRAVEL LIBRARY

Edited by Paul Zach

Times Editions, 422 Thomson Road
Singapore 1129
© Copyright by Times Editions, 1988

Printed by Tien Wah Press, Singapore
Color separated by Far East Offset, Kuala Lumpur
Typeset by Superskill Graphics, Singapore

Cover: Taipei lit up for the Double Ten (October 10th)
festival, celebrating the 1911 overthrow of the Manchu
rulers and their Ching Dynasty.
Endpapers: Taipei's Presidential Office Building decorated
and lit up at night for the Double Ten celebration. The
Double Ten rebellion marked the birth of the Republic of
China. The three colors of the Republican flag, visible here,
represent Dr Sun Yat Sen's Three Principles of the People.
Frontispiece: Crowds walk through the huge white gate
leading to the square facing the Chung-cheng Memorial
Hall. The Hall is dedicated to the memory of the late
President Chiang Kai-shek, leader of the Republic of
China for half a century.

ISBN: 981-204-005-6

TAIPEI

Photographed by Ian Lloyd
Text by Paul Mooney

Designed by Leonard Lueras

First Edition 1988

TIMES EDITIONS

The Chung-cheng Memorial Hall, shown here in a night scene, is dedicated to the memory of Chiang Kai-shek, leader of the Republic of China for half a century. **Following pages:** The towering memorial hall exemplifies the grandest traditions of classical Chinese architecture. The white marble structure stands 70 meters tall and is the largest building in Taiwan. High school students parading in their military-like uniforms hold portraits of Sun Yat-sen, who led the movement to overthrow the Ching Dynasty early this century. A crowd of onlookers examines an extremely long dragon, used in the dragon dance held on auspicious occasions. Brightly colored shop signs line a street in Taipei. At night these signs give a carnival atmosphere to the city.

Contents

Taipei

Modern Hub of an Ancient Culture

U pon arriving in Taipei, newcomers often develop an instant case of mixed feelings. At first sight, the city doesn't look the part of the dynamic, ultra-modern hub of unbridled development it's often cracked up to be, the way that Singapore does. Nor does it boast the traditional charm and timeless character found in other parts of Asia. It can hardly be described as exotic; unlike Bangkok, there are no floating markets; unlike Bali, there are no sarong-clad natives balancing fruit on their head. Furthermore, nothing in Taipei remotely compares to the dramatic romantic harbor view of Hong Kong that can be seen from Victoria Peak.

Still, there is something attractive about Taipei. Exactly what it is is difficult to put into words. That's because there is no one thing that reaches out and grabs you. On the contrary, Taipei is the kind of city that you have to reach out and grab.

You'll have to be quick to catch it, though. Taipei has been called the fastest growing city in Asia. While its ambitious residents strive to retain some vestiges of their past, Taipei has in fact found itself being propelled so fast into the future that no one is quite sure exactly what the blend of new and old should look like. Thus, the city has an unfortunate veneer of looking like it is neither a charming enclave of typical Chinese architecture, art and culture nor a modern, state-of-the-art metropolis. However, visitors willing to invest a little effort into scratching the surface and looking into the heart of the city will discover it still has a lot to offer.

Historically, Taipei is relatively new — in every respect. Even its site developed rather late by the geological yardstick. The city, including suburbs, occupies a triangular basin that measures 20.5 kilometers (13 miles) from east to west and 28 kilometers (18 miles) from north to south. The basin is actually a tectonic depression that was a huge lake during the Archaean Age some four billion years ago. Only after millenniums of geological evolution did the depression become alluvial.

In time, the lake gradually disappeared as a result of an uplifting of the earth's crust in the area. However, scholars say that the center of the basin was still waterlogged as recently as AD 1697. A century ago, much of the downtown area in the central part of the city was still muddy paddy fields.

Chinese histories dating back to before the Han Dynasty (BC 206 – AD 221) refer to a place that was probably Taiwan. But no one is

quite sure when people began settling in the Taipei basin. What is known is that large numbers of Chinese left the mainland and began sailing across the Taiwan Strait during the Ming Dynasty (1368-1644). Records show that Chinese boats from the mainland first sailed to the Tamsui River to fish and trade in 1521. However, the Chinese emperors paid little attention to the island until Europeans began to show an interest in the 17th Century.

In 1624, the Dutch East India Company established a base on Taiwan near the present day city of Tainan, on the southwest coast. Tainan later became the capital of the island and remained so until the 19th Century. Two

Standing at attention, this high school marching band (left) is participating in the annual Double Ten ceremony. The image of Dr Sun Yat-sen dominates the scene. Another group (above) participates in an International Lion's Club Parade.

15

years after the Dutch arrived, the Spanish attempted to plant a foothold on the island. But the Dutch managed to drive their colonial rivals out in 1641.

One of the most colorful characters in the history of Taiwan arrived on the island with his fleet of ships in 1661. Cheng Cheng-kung, who the West came to know as Koxinga, was the son of a Chinese pirate and a Japanese mother. Koxinga was a patriot loyal to the

ordered to reclaim land along the banks of the river as far as Chihlansanpo.

When the Chinese came from the mainland they sailed up the Tamsui River, which flows into the Taiwan Strait, and first settled in Hsinchuang where they established a farming community. In 1709 reclamation was extended from Hsinchuang, today a veritable suburb about 30 minutes from the city center, to Mongka (present-day Wanhua), the first

Ming Dynasty, which at the time was under attack by Manchu invaders. He drove out the Dutch and used the island as a base from which he attempted to recapture mainland China from the Manchus. Although Koxinga was ultimately unsuccessful in that endeavor, his followers managed to hold out against the Manchus until 1683.

Perhaps more importantly, at least in the history of Taiwan, Koxinga laid the foundations for the development of Taipei. In 1661, he assigned one of his generals, Huang An, to command the army and naval forces at Tamsui, along the Tamsui River, northeast of the present capital. Huang's soldiers were later

Soldiers demonstrate precision drill movements during the change of the honor guard at the National Revolutionary Martyr's Shrine, just northeast of the Grand Hotel. National service is compulsory for all able-bodied young men.

Chinese community complete with temples and businesses in the heart of modern Taipei.

At that time, the Tamsui was wide and deep and ships could easily navigate up and down the river. The early Chinese settlers of the area rowed across to the opposite bank to trade with the island's indigenous aborigines who brought their produce there in dugouts. Since so many canoes crowded the river at that spot, the place soon became known as Mongka which literally means "canoe" in one of the aboriginal languages. The name was eventually adopted by both the aborigines and the Chinese traders to refer to the entire area.

Expansion continued gradually at first. In 1737, the city spread to encompass the Wenshan and Sungshan sections. By this time, Mongka had already become a prosperous center of trade with a large community. In 1737, the inhabitants erected the Lungshan, or

"Dragon Mountain," Temple in honor of the Goddess of Mercy. Today it remains one of Taiwan's most popular temples.

By 1853, Mongka had reached the peak of its prosperity. Ships crowded its port and thousands of shops and trading firms lined its streets. Around this time the area also developed a certain notoriety for licentious nightlife that still exists.

By the turn of the century, Mongka had

entered a period of decline because it became impossible for ships to enter the port. The first obstruction was a sandbar which developed about 100 years ago. As the Tamsui River became increasingly shallow, ships could no longer freely sail in and out of Mongka. A second factor was the building of a railway bridge at what is known today as Tachiaotou. This bridge had much the same effect as the sandbar — it prevented ships from sailing into the area. Although the railway bridge was later converted into a drawbridge, much of the business had already relocated to other places.

Between 1879 and 1882, a wall was built around "old Taipei;" it ran 15,000 meters around the city, was 15 meters tall and 12 meters thick. An artillery turret to discourage attacks topped each gate.

China made Taiwan a province in 1886. Its first governor, Liu Ming-chuan, transferred the seat of the capital from Tainan in the south to Taipei in the north. A noted reformer, Liu immediately began setting up railroad, postal and telegraphic services. A year after his arrival, Liu turned on the first electric light making Taipei the first city in all of China to be electrified. In 1889, China's first train made its maiden trip from Taipei to Keelung.

Taiwan was ceded to Japan in 1895 following China's defeat in the Sino-Japanese War. Foreshadowing future developments, a group of literati in Taipei, known as the Peony Poet's Club, reacted by declaring the establishment of a Republic of Taiwan. Although Japan's superior military might soon defeated the independence movement, sporadic fighting continued for years.

The Japanese made Taipei the seat of their government in Taiwan prompting an immediate change in the city's appearance. The first thing to go was the wall. In 1900 workers began tearing it down to make way for an expansion program. It took them 11 years to demolish almost all of it. Only four of the original five gates remain standing today. In order to enable traffic to move past them unimpeded, the gates have been made the centerpieces of busy traffic circles.

Ironically, European-style buildings were another legacy of Japanese rule. Many are still in use today as government offices. To their credit, the Japanese made major investments in infrastructure projects as well. They expanded the railway system, built roads and extended telegraph lines. They also established banking and currency systems.

But the humbling aspect of the occupation was the attempt to "Japanize" local society. The Japanese generals outlawed footbinding and forced men to cut off their queues, the pigtail hairstyle worn by all men during the Ching Dynasty (1644-1911). Schools were opened that promulgated the Japanese language and customs and people were expected to wear either Japanese or Western clothing. In fact, the teaching of written Chinese was expressly prohibited in schools.

As subjects of Japan, Taiwan's people were even expected to fight for the Rising Sun. During World War II, the Japanese drafted 200,000 Taiwanese into their military. Many were sent to fight in Southeast Asia and some 30,000 died in action. As a whole, however, the people of Taiwan did not suffer under the Japanese as much as their mainland Chinese brothers across the strait where even civilians endured brutal treatment.

Today many of those educated in the Japanese school system still retain certain Japanese habits and still enjoy speaking the language. Some even look back upon the 50-year occupation as the "good old days."

Indeed, during an interview with an elderly Taiwanese couple in Taipei, one foreign reporter discovered Japanese books and knickknacks around their house. The couple explained that they had been educated in

hot sulfur baths. It was a popular Japanese spa during the colonial period and still attracts a lot of Japanese tourists, particularly men who come to relax with the town's plethora of pretty hostesses.

One of the last traces of the occupation are the 5,000 Japanese-style houses erected during that time. Many of these interesting houses with their tatami mats, sliding doors and gardens can still be found clustered in parts of

Japanese schools in Taiwan and that they still corresponded and even visited with some of their former teachers and their families.

When asked if they felt more Chinese or Japanese, the couple quickly answered, "Oh, Chinese, of course." But when they showed the reporter to the door they bowed low and politely, in the manner of the Japanese.

Peitou, a lovely niche of a suburb, is set in a rocky volcanic site just 30 minutes northwest of Taipei. Its atmosphere demands that the visitor make the brief trip there by taxi, preferably via the lovely winding roads of Yangming Mountain. Peitou has dozens of wonderful Japanese-style inns and hotels with

Taipei. But unfortunately, many are being razed to make way for tall buildings and probably will not survive into the next century.

Chow Yu, the owner of the popular Wisteria Teahouse, went to court in 1985 in an attempt to keep the government from tearing down the beautiful Japanese house which he grew up in as a boy and which now serves as a teahouse. Chow argues that these buildings are an architectural asset that should be restored.

Japanese rule over Taiwan ended with Japan's defeat in World War II. In 1945, the island was returned to Chinese rule. When the mainland fell to the Mao Tse-tung's communists in 1949, the Nationalist government fled to Taiwan with an estimated two million mainlanders, including a half-million soldiers. The Nationalists made Taipei the temporary capital of the Republic of China in December 1949, marking a new phase in the island's development.

A crowd of worshipers jam the Taoist Hsing Tien Temple, Taipei's most crowded, to worship Kuan Kong, a legendary hero and the patron saint of businessmen (above). A large incense and paper charm urn stands in the center.

18

Still, Taipei remained a backwater town for the next two decades. Its residents still relied on pedicabs for transportation even as late as the middle of the 1960s. This gradually began changing later that same decade, however, when the economy started taking off.

Thus, Taipei began making the transition from a small functional town to a large cosmopolitan city. When the Nationalist government withdrew to Taiwan in 1949 following

the communist takeover of the mainland, the island's future looked bleak. Inflation was rampant, unemployment was high, production was down, the government had no money and natural resources were limited.

Then, President Chiang Kai-shek with economic assistance from the United States, embarked on a program of economic reforms that were later to transform the island into one of the fastest growing economies in the world. By 1965, American aid which had averaged $100 million annually since 1951, ended as the economy began to take off. Just three years later the trade balance, which previously had been in favor of the United States, began to tilt in favor of Taiwan and the island, one-third the size of the American state of Virginia, now ranks among the world's top twenty trading nations.

The economy has expanded at an average

rate of 10 per cent annually from the late 1960s to the present decade; today there are 101.5 television sets, 96.3 refrigerators and 76.9 telephones for each 100 households. One of the most obvious examples of the island's wealth is the number of Mercedes Benz's and other expensive automobiles parked in front of the city's finer restaurants and stores.

With such a dynamic economy, Taipei naturally offered an increasing number of job

opportunities, medical facilities and schools. More and more young people from rural areas began migrating to the city, attracted by the glitter of modernity and the promise of a better future. The Japanese designed Taipei to comfortably accommodate about 600,000 people; Taipei's population was 400,000 in 1945. But by 1963, it had climbed past the million mark and in 1975 more than doubled again. The rapid growth spurred demand for more housing and office space. Surrounded by mountains, Taipei had only one way to go and that was up. In 1978 the ban on highrise and hotel construction was lifted. Between 1974 and 1985, 53,339 new buildings went up.

*A **brass bearded soldier**, possibly a member of a northern "barbarian" group, (**above left**) supports the upper part of a temple incense burner. Candles are lit in many temples (**above right**). The central candle carries the Chinese character for peace.*

Historical Chronology

1521 – Boats from mainland China sail into the Tamsui River to fish and trade.

1624 – The Dutch East India Company begins to establish bases in Taiwan.

1661 – Koxinga, the Ming Dynasty loyalist, arrives in Taiwan.

1662 – Koxinga defeats the Dutch and forces them from the island.

1683 – The Manchus, who overthrew the Ming Dynasty in China in 1644, defeat Ming loyalists in Taiwan and bring the island under their control.

1684 – Taiwan is made a prefecture of Fukien province.

1709 – Chen Lai-chang, an immigrant from Chuan-chow, Fukien province, extends the farming area from Hsinchuang to Mongka. Many people from his province settle in the area.

1737 – Mongka (present-day Wanhua) becomes a prosperous center of trade in the Taipei basin.

1738 – The Lungshan Temple is built.

1815 – A strong earthquake destroys the Mongka area and the Lungshan Temple.

1853 – Mongka becomes a prosperous port crowded with ships bringing in merchandise to cope with the needs of its burgeoning population.

1879 – Work begins on gates and a wall that runs 15,000 meters around Taipei City.

1883 – The wall is completed making Taipei City a veritable fortress.

1884 – French forces seize the Pescadores, a group of small offshore islands, blockade Taiwan and occupy Keelung.

1885 – Liu Ming-chuan is appointed the first Chinese governor of Taiwan and establishes his government in Taipei.

1886 – Taiwan is made a province of China and Governor Liu makes Taipei the capital.

1887 – Governor Liu switches on the first light bulb in Taipei, making it the first city in China to be electrified. Liu introduces modern mines, improves harbor works and establishes overseas cable connections. Under his rule, Taiwan becomes the most progressive province in China.

1889 – China's first train makes a trip from Taipei to the port city of Keelung.

1895 – Taiwan is ceded to Japan following China's defeat in the Sino-Japanese War and Taipei is made the seat of the Japanese governor's office. The Japanese prohibit foot-binding, opium smoking and the wearing of queues. For the next decade, Taiwanese guerrilla groups keep pressure on Japanese military forces.

1897 – An area within the city walls is cleared and drained to make way for the construction of a Japanese "town" of shops, offices and homes.

1898 – A typhoon hits Taipei, swelling the Tamsui River to a height of 22 feet within a few hours. The strong winds and torrential rains destroy more than 3,000 buildings and other structures as river water spreads throughout the city.

1899 – Taipei's New Park is built.

1900 – The Japanese begin dismantling the city wall and the West Gate, but the task takes 11 years. The other gates are left standing.

1903 – Taiwan's first hydroelectric generators are put into service at the headwaters of the Hsintien River. This new source of energy is the catalyst for small industries that begin springing up in and around Taipei.

1919 – The Japanese build the President's Office, which serves as the Governor-General's Office during the Occupation.

1928 – In Taipei, the Japanese establish Taihoku Imperial University, Taiwan's first institution of higher learning.

1940 – The Taipei train station is built by the Japanese administration.

1943 – Franklin D. Roosevelt, Winston Churchill, and Chiang Kai-shek meet in Cairo and declare that when World War II ends Japan will be stripped of all of its occupied territories including Taiwan which will be restored to the Republic of China.

1944 – American planes bomb major cities in Taiwan. Thousands of people move from the city to the hills or country homes. Some 18,000 Taipei residents are made homeless when the Japanese cut wide fire lanes between crowded Twatutia and the heart of the city. Winds blowing from the west spare Mongka and Twatutia as repeated U.S. air raids spark big fires in the city's administrative district.

1945 – Japan's surrender ends World War II and closes the book on 50 years of Japanese rule as Taiwan is returned to Chinese control. Japan's Taihoku Imperial University is renamed National Taiwan University.

1947 – An estimated 10,000 native Taiwanese are massacred by Nationalist soldiers after anti-government rioting.

1949 – The Nationalist government, overpowered by Chinese communists on the mainland, retreats to Taiwan and makes Taipei the temporary capital of the Republic of China.

1950 – Chiang Kai-shek resumes the Presidency in Taipei in March. In June, U.S. President Harry Truman orders the U.S. Seventh Fleet to prevent a Communist attack against Taiwan and at the same time asks the Nationalist government to cease air and sea operations against the mainland.

1962 – The Taiwan Stock Exchange is opened in Taipei and the first commercial television station goes on the air.

1963 – Tropical Typhoon Gloria lashes northern Taiwan resulting in 200 deaths.

1967 – Taipei is made a special municipality under the jurisdiction of the Executive Yuan with status equal to that of a province. Six satellite townships and rural districts are incorporated into the city, expanding its area to 272.14 square kilometers.

1974 – As the city's boundaries are swelled by new arrivals from rural areas, the population climbs to more than two million.

1975 – President Chiang Kai-shek, the long-time leader of the Republic of China, passes away in Taipei at the age of 88, his dream of regaining control over mainland China unfulfilled. His son, Chiang Ching-kuo, assumes control of the government, ushering in some new policies.

1978 – Protesters demonstrate outside the U.S. Embassy in Taipei after Washington announces it will establish diplomatic relations with the communist People's Republic of China and cuts ties with Taiwan's Nationalist government.

1979 – The U.S. Embasssy in Taipei is closed as the United States formerly inaugurates diplomatic relations with Peking. The 28-year-old U.S. military presence in Taiwan also comes to a close as Rear Admiral James Linder, commander of the U.S. Taiwan Defense Command, leaves Taipei.

1980 – The monolithic Chiang Kai-shek Memorial Hall in downtown Taipei is opened to the public. Fort San Domingo in Tamsui, built by the Spanish in 1628 and later leased to the British, is returned to Chinese control as the 113-year lease expires.

1983 – A groundbreaking ceremony is held to mark the beginning of construction on Taipei's US$600 million underground railway project.

1985 – Taipei's first test tube baby is born at the Veteran's General Hospital.

1986 – Opposition politicians defy the government ban on the formation of new political parties to establish the Democratic Progressive Party at the Grand Hotel in Taipei.

1988 – President Chiang Ching-kuo, son of the late Generalissimo Chiang Kai-shek, dies in Taipei. Chiang's death brings to an end more than 40 years of Chiang family leadership of the Republic of China, which began on the mainland and ends on Taiwan. Hundreds of thousands of citizens wait in line for hours at the Martyr's Shrine to pay their last respects to the President who carried out a wide range of far-reaching political and economic reforms during his term in office. Vice-President Lee Teng-hui, concensus choice as Chiang's successor, became the Republic's first locally-born President.

While most of today's wealthy Taiwanese businessmen are descendants of former large landowners, there are plenty of rags-to-riches tales. Chang Yung-fa, for example, started out as a clerk on a tramp steamer and worked his way up to ship's captain. In 1968, he'd saved enough money to buy himself a secondhand ship. From that humble beginning, he built the Evergreen Marine fleet of 63 vessels, the largest container ship company in

and 600,000 motorcycles that all seem to be plying the city's streets simultaneously. They compete for space on the inadequate street grid with more than 30,000 taxi drivers.

Modernization has also increased pollution. In fact, the air has gotten so bad that people often ride motorcycles and bicycles with their faces partially concealed by surgical masks in an attempt to lessen the amount of airborne toxins they inhale. The Tamsui River, which

the world. Chang's personal fortune now exceeds U.S. $1 billion.

As a growing city, Taipei naturally offered increasing numbers of job opportunities. The job structure moved from agriculture to industry. So more and more young people from rural areas began shifting to the city, attracted not only by the promise of work but the city's contemporary veneer.

Modernization of the city has had its good and bad points. As in many other Asian capitals, vehicular traffic is completely out-of-control. Few people owned cars in the mid-1970s, but the island's recent affluence has spawned a plague of more than 250,000 cars

Lay volunteers, their hands folded piously, read scriptures inside the Hsing Tien Temple (above), as worshipers burn offerings in the courtyard. At other times temples can be a setting for quiet contemplation (right) or neighborhood meetings.

was pristine and lovely when the first Chinese settlers from the mainland sailed up it centuries ago, is also seriously polluted. Ironically, that is credited with saving a life: according to local newspaper reports one woman who attempted to commit suicide by jumping in and drowning herself several years ago, swam to safety complaining that the murky water was "a fate worse than death."

Visitors who return to Taipei after only a few year's absence are often shocked that the city has changed so much in so short a time. Most impressive is the fast-growing "East Side," especially in the vicinity of Chung Hsiao East Road known among some expatriates as the "New Ginza." Fifteen years ago, much of the area was still paddy where rice was grown. Now it has hundreds of sleek, modern buildings and the streets bustle with businessmen, shoppers and fun-seekers.

The Lungshan Temple, symbol of Taipei's traditional religion, is a popular venue for rallies and opera performances. Auspicious dragons ride the roof, flanking the central "pearl of potentiality", which represents the sun.

Taipei's Timeless Temple

In 1885 when French Marines were preparing to attack Taipei, the residents of Mongka organized a volunteer unit to help defend the city. The official emblem carried into battle by this battalion was the image of the Lungshan Temple.

The fact that a rendering of the temple was adopted as the battle emblem is not surprising. Built in 1738 when Mongka was at the peak of its prosperity, the temple quickly became the center of the area's religious, social, commercial and even judicial affairs. And thriving businesses grew nearby.

Before long, the temple's reputation was known throughout the island and it became a magnet for worshipers from all over the island. Today, it ranks as one of the oldest and largest of the more than 5,000 temples and shrines on Taiwan and is considered one of the best examples of traditional Chinese temple architecture.

The roots of Lungshan, which literally means "Dragon Mountain" in English, can be traced back to Fukien province on mainland China. In the early days when businessmen were plying between the mainland and Taiwan, a merchant from Chuanchow in Fukien traveled to Taiwan. While passing by the site where the temple was later to be constructed, the merchant stopped to urinate. In order to avoid committing a sacrilege, he removed the sacred incense pouch that hung around his neck and placed it on a stalk of bamboo. The pouch came from the Lungshan Temple in Chuanchow and the merchant wore it everywhere he went. This time, however, he absentmindedly left it hanging on the branch.

As the story goes, people in the area noticed a

bright light shining among the bamboo and were frightened. Soon their curiosity got the best of them, though, and they decided to take a closer look. When they reached the area they discovered the pouch, which was inscribed with the words, "This pouch of incense ash originated from the Goddess of Mercy of the Lungshan Temple."

Believing the shining pouch to be a miracle sent from the gods, the people spread the word of its existence, attracting scores of pilgrims. The inspired locals decided to erect a shrine on the spot, an exact replica of the temple in Chuanchow, dedicated to the Goddess of Mercy. They laboriously brought in every piece of timber and stone used in its construction from Fukien. Not a single nail or drop of glue was used. Instead the pieces were expertly fitted together according to traditional architectural principles. Within three years, the Temple was completed.

During the next 200 years, the temple was damaged four times. The first incident occurred in 1815 when an earthquake leveled the Mongka area, including the temple. According to reports from that time, the statue of the Goddess of Mercy survived untouched and remained on its pedestal amid the surrounding devastation. News of this miracle attracted even more pilgrims.

The temple was damaged again in 1867 when a strong typhoon slammed into the island. Craftsmen managed to restore the temple, aspiring to emulate the original design using the same materials whenever possible. But by 1919 it was falling victim to an even more destructive enemy — age. Its paintings were fading and wooden beams were rotting.

Craftsmen repaired the damage and made the temple sturdier to help it better withstand the vicissitudes of time and nature. What its caretakers didn't know, though, was that the temple would soon face the destructive might of man and machine.

On June 8, 1945, as the end of World War II approached, Allied planes bombed the Mongka area where Japanese troops were billeted and hit the main hall of the Lungshan Temple. The temple was destroyed; anything that managed to survive the initial blast was reduced to ash by the ensuing fire. The flames from the incendiary bomb were so strong that they melted the iron railings surrounding the camphorwood statue of the Goddess of Mercy. Once again, however, the statue itself remained unscathed on the main altar amid the temple ruins.

Although the Wanhua area is no longer as economically, socially, or culturally important as in years past, the Lungshan Temple persists as a stronghold of Taiwanese traditionalism. It continues to be the hub of religious and secular activities. Worshipers crowd through its gates every night and neighborhood residents sit in the courtyard every evening relaxing and chatting with friends.

Fashionable stores like Ralph Lauren and Charles Jourdan do a brisk business selling the latest, most expensive fashions from Europe, Japan and the United States, while posh restaurants, coffee shops and piano bars successfully push nouvelle cuisine, espresso and Irish coffee.

Chung Hsiao East has also grown into a fast-food jungle. Almost every major Western franchise has at least one store in the area. McDonald's, Wendy's, Pizza Hut, Mr. Donut, Kentucky Fried Chicken and Baskin Robbins are all within five minutes of each other in the Ding Hao area of Chung Hsiao East Road. Although the residents of some foreign cities have fought against the proliferation of fast food restaurants in their neighborhoods, the people of Taipei have welcomed them as a sign of their new economic status and changing life-style. Indeed, word that a fast-food outlet is about to be built somewhere never fails to drive up property prices in the vicinity.

Each day, young, well-dressed people, wearing the latest hairstyles and clothes, while away hours in Dairy Queen and Hardy's sipping cokes and chatting with their friends. Students also find the restaurants a convenient place for doing homework after school and on weekends. Fast-food not only attracts the young, however. Conservatively-dressed senior citizens are often seen munching away on fries and hamburgers. Indeed, one distinguished-looking former Chinese ambassador frequently dines at McDonald's Yung-kang branch on Hsinyi Road. Even Buddhist monks have been seen entering Pizza Hut, presumably to sample the vegetarian supreme.

In view of the fact that the Chinese are at least as chauvinistic about their food as the French, the fast-food phenomenon has come as a surprise. What's not surprising is that some Chinese entrepreneurs are studying the science of foreign fast food and adapting its efficient, money-making management methods to the local food industry. Powei Siang, for instance, is a Taiwanese restaurant that serves up fish-ball soup, sticky rice wrapped in bamboo leaves, as well as Coca-cola and coffee, over-the-counter from an aluminum-lined kitchen on Hsinyi Road. Another McDonald's look-alike, Hsiangji Cheng (Mandarin for "Chicken City") dishes out fried chicken and french fries.

Ju Ming, Taipei's most famous contemporary sculptor, wields his axe on wood with the same combination of power and delicacy that guides a Chinese calligrapher's brush. This work depicts a pose from the Tai Chi Chuan form of martial arts.

Raiders of the Lost Art

Many of the more than 600,000 pieces housed in the National Palace Museum on Taipei's outskirts are priceless masterpieces; together they comprise what is arguably the world's greatest collection of Chinese art. Furthermore, the story of the collection's long, arduous journey to Taiwan is one of the world's great tales. Before the bulk of the items arrived in Taiwan in 1948 when the Chinese Communists were completing their takeover of the mainland, the collection was carted over mountains, across rivers, and up and down the country's roads on a journey filled with so much intrigue and adventure, it reads like the script of Raiders of the Lost Ark.

The origins of the collection date back to the Sung Dynasty (960-1279) when Emperor Tai-tsung instructed officials to search for outstanding paintings and calligraphy. The mass of art they brought back gradually grew to include porcelain, carvings, enamelware, lacquerware, books, jade and more; but down through the ages only emperors, their courts, and high officials were permitted to gaze upon these wonders.

After the revolution of 1911 which resulted in the overthrow of the Ching Dynasty, the victors permitted Henry Pu Yi, the last surviving Manchu emperor, to continue living in the Forbidden City. However, in 1924, the Nationalist government suddenly gave the deposed emperor 24 hours to move out. When he had gone experts began cataloging the entire palace collection, a monumental task that took two years. In October 1925, the government exhibited these treasures of Chinese culture to the public for the first time.

When the Mukden Incident occurred on September 18, 1931, officials realized that it was only a matter of time before war reached Peking so they began making plans to move the most valuable pieces from the path of advancing Japanese soldiers. Thus on the evening of February 5, 1933, wheelbarrows started shuttling back and forth between the Forbidden City and the train station. Some 19,557 crates were moved, marking the beginning of a 16-year odyssey — and one of the most exciting episodes in the history of art.

Officials requisitioned two entire trains for the trip to Pukou, across the river from Nanking. There officials waited a month before they received instructions to load the crates on a ship bound for Shanghai where they were stored in a warehouse.

Within four years, the collection was again transferred, this time to a new temperature-controlled facility in Nanking. But before workers had time to even consider putting the collection on display, the Marco Polo Incident occurred on July 7, 1937; that brought the threat of war to Shanghai and Nanking and once again endangered the collection.

Just before the two cities fell, the collection was again on the move. Eighty boxes that were shipped to the library at Hunan University in Changsha barely escaped destruction on two occasions: Shortly after the crates arrived, that city's train station was bombed. And anxious workers hurriedly shipped the treasure to Kueiyang just one day before bombs leveled the university library.

In Kueiyang officials involved in the complex job of keeping track of the collection's movements decided to try storing some of the crates in underground caves, but workers soon realized the dampness could be damaging. Then orders came to move the crates to Hanchung. But because there was no railway line, trucks had to be used. They had to make 300 trips to transport 7,000 crates across snow-swept roads in the dead of winter. At times, the snow fell so hard and heavily that drivers were unable to see the road. Forty-eight days later, the objects arrived in Hanchung. Just as the treasures' guardians learned that the caves where they had been stored in in Kueiyang had been destroyed, their intended home in Hanchung was also bombed.

The next destination was Chengtu province, some 525 kilometers (326 miles) and five bridgeless rivers away. It took 10 months to complete the arduous

journey; several trucks that overturned along the way never did make it. Miraculously, not a single item was damaged in transit. In Chengtu the story was the same, however; bombs blasted the city of Chungking and the crates had to be moved 150 kilometers (93 miles) southwest to Omei. There they remained until the war ended in 1945.

Meanwhile, another batch of crates was shipped by boat to Hankow just as the Japanese marched into Nanking and the city was in a state of confusion. Later 10,000 more crates were shipped to Chungking but rerouted to Losan after the bombing. While ferrying across the river one of the vessel's tow ropes broke loose sending it to what seemed to be a certain crate-splintering collision on the rocks. Fortunately, the ship ran aground on a comparatively cushiony spit of sand instead.

The collection survived that incident and was eventually packed up in Chungking and transported to Nanjing in 1947. According to accounts of the voyage, one crew member spent the entire three-month trip on his hands and knees fighting off termites that had begun licking their chops when the crates were loaded aboard. On December 9, 1947 the collection was deposited in the Nanjing Museum where the first exhibition in quite some time was held the following year.

Within a year, however, the collection was again uprooted when Communist Chinese forces turned the tide against the Nationalist goverment. In November, 1948, the boxes of art were packed onto three ships for the journey to Taiwan. Even then 700 boxes had to be left behind in the harbor to make room for refugees anxiously seeking to board these last ships.

The bulk of the collection made it to Keelung in February, 1949 and was stowed away in caves in Taichung until it was once and for all moved to its ultimate destination, the National Palace Museum in Taipei, when construction was completed in 1965. All in all, it had traveled about 10,000 kilometers (6,240 miles) over a period of 32 years from the day it first left the Forbidden City in 1933. Incredibly, not a single piece had been damaged during the ordeal.

Once the collection was safely in its new home, museum caretakers faced new threats, though: the fragile, irreplaceable items had to be protected against fire, theft, extremes in temperature, humidity and pollution. So huge is the collection that it is impossible to exhibit all at once, so the items on display are displayed on a rotating basis. Those that are not on exhibit are stored in custom-made silk and cotton-lined boxes in temperature-controlled tunnels in the mountain behind the main building.

In 1985 the museum's curators installed upgraded storage facilities including a U.S.$3 million security system. It constantly monitors and records all activity inside and outside the vault with all-weather infra-red and microwave scanners. Only specialists are granted entrance and only to areas for which they are responsible. The storeroom also has an automatic fire extinguishing system that uses special gases to protect items that could be damaged by water.

Great care is also taken to ensure proper lighting and temperature and humidity conditions, which differ depending on the sensitivities of each type of artifacts. Visiting art experts who receive permission to examine a certain piece are required to take special precautions. Not only are they prohibited from handling silk items, but they are even barred from speaking while wearing a surgical mask to ensure that human breath is not allowed to contaminate any of the precious material.

The 600,000 pieces of art housed in the museum constitute the cream of the more than one million items once stored in Peking's Imperial Palace. However, few people have been fortunate enough to have ever viewed the entire collection. There is only enough space to exhibit 15,000 pieces simultaneously and exhibits are rotated every three to six months. At that rate, even if you make several trips to the museum annually it would take more than ten years to view all of the pieces!

To appreciate and comprehend the more traditionally-Chinese side of Taipei takes time and effort. Many of the city's most fascinating sites can be discovered by wandering through the small side streets, markets and old sections of the city, areas that are increasingly falling under the menacing shadows of high-rises.Shops on an estimated 3,000 streets in Taipei specialize in selling related merchandise, everything from clothes to

During a walk down Tihua Street, you will see and smell all sorts of herbs, remedies, antidotes, concoctions, and the usual large assortment of aphrodisiacal potions for which the Chinese are legendary. A hard and bitter apple-like fruit called the medlar, juniper berry, antlers, dried lizards, and scorpion tails are all neatly filed away in dozens of tiny drawer's behind the druggist's counter.

During the Ching Dynasty, ships sailed up

Chinese herbs. Such thoroughfares are important because they play an important role in Taipei's social and economic life. For example, Taoyuan Street has developed a reputation for its noodle stands, Amoy Street for shoes, Hsi Yuan Street for Buddhist icons, and Chungking South Road for books.

Tihua Street, located in the Yenping district, is one of the oldest in Taipei and as yet has been untouched by the rapid change occurring just a few blocks away. Many of the Tihua area's old businesses operate out of old red brick buildings that still line the streets. It is known primarily as a center for the sale of dried goods and Chinese herbal medicines.

The American influence shows in Taipei, in a hotel foyer display (right). These uniformed high school students stand in front of Mai Dang Lao's, also known as McDonald's (above). America is a popular destination for Taipei's university students.

the Tamsui River and unloaded their goods in the port near Tihua Street. Governor Liu Ming-chuan set the section aside as a residential area for foreign businessmen and it gradually developed into a wholesale center.

Following the retreat of the Nationalist Party and its troops to Taiwan in the 1940s, the government restricted all contact with the Chinese communists. But officials realized that people relied on Chinese herbs, many of which cannot be grown in Taiwan, so the government decided to allow herbs from the mainland to be brought to the island through middlemen in Hong Kong. Tihua Street has been the center of the trade ever since and people from all over the island shop here.

Another fascinating aspect of the district is its unique architectural style, known as the *kulanyu.* When Fukienese merchants traveled to Southeast Asia, many were impressed with

the rococo style of the colonial buildings. Upon their return to China, they combined that style with southern architecture in a hybrid that eventually developed into the *kulanyu* style. The Chinese merchants who migrated to Taipei brought the same building style to Tihua Street. Lee Chian Lang, a professor of architecture at Chinese Culture University and author of many books on the subject, sees this as significant: "Architecture

is a reflection of culture. The merchants of Tihua Street did business with many people and this is reflected in their architecture.

Not far from Tihua Street lies the Hsimenting, or West Gate, area. Although the Japanese tore down the gate in the early 1900s, the area has retained that old moniker. In recent years, Hsimenting has acquired a reputation for being the Times Square of Taipei. Wu Chang Street, also known as Movie Street, houses numerous cinemas and the facades of many of the area's buildings are usually wall-papered with enormous movie posters, some several stories high, that are colorful but occasionally grotesque.

A Chinese herbalist examines preserved ginseng roots (above). Most of the herbal medicine sold in Taipei is brought from the mainland through Hong Kong middlemen. Buyers hunt for bargains (right) at the Kwanghwa Jade Market, open every Sunday.

A young craftsman assembles a large bamboo steamer at one of the few cooperage shops in Taipei **(below).** Though the arrival of plastics put many such businesses out of operation, crafts are now enjoying a comeback.

Hooked on Wood

Visitors strolling among the fashionable shops and offices on Chung Shan North Road occasionally stumble upon an improbable establishment known as the Lin Tien Cooperage. One of the first questions they ask proprietor Lin Hsiang-lin is just how long he has been in business there. Lin proudly points to the old clock hanging high on the wall; 1928 is painted on its dust-covered face, commemorating the year his father opened the shop in an era when craftsmanship was still valued.

Incongruously located in the chic district at the foot of the Fu Hsing Bridge, the Lin Tien Cooperage is a thriving reminder of old Taipei. Its worn brick wall is pockmarked from decades of being hit with tools and buckets, the dark bamboo stairs at the back have been worn smooth from millions of footsteps and the rough, uneven floor is covered with fresh wood shavings. The 60 square-foot shop is piled high with wooden buckets and pails, leaving Lin barely enough space to work.

Cooperage is the craft of making and mending casks, barrels and other items of wood. Back in 1928, wooden utensils were commonly used in most Taiwanese homes for everything from taking a bath and washing clothes to cooking rice and carrying night soil. In those days, the street was lined with cooperages and business was so good that the Lin Tien employed five busy workers who labored for 'ong hours.

Lin Hsiang-lin was born in 1929 and at the age of 13 was sent by his father to the port city of Keelung, north of Taipei, to serve as an apprentice to a master craftsman who trained him in the arts of the cooper. Three years later, in 1945, young Lin returned to Taipei to help his father run the shop, just as the Japanese were surrendering and the Nationalist government returned to power in Taiwan marking the start of Taipei's economic boom.

Business remained good until the early 1960s when plastic, washing machines, electric rice cookers and modern bathroom furnishings became popular in Taiwan, replacing almost all of the old wooden utensils that Lin prided himself on creating. As neighborhood competitors shut down one after the other, Lin tenaciously held on, gradually letting go of his workers, but refusing to give up the trade he'd practiced for so many years.

Although he struggled through bad times, his perserverance has paid off. In recent years, the reviving nostalgic interest in preservation and the past has given Lin's business a new lease on life. And as one of the few remaining cooperages left in Taiwan, Lin has no problem attracting buyers from all over the island.

Many customers consider Lin's wooden buckets works of art, but they still have utilitarian value as well. Among his best-selling items are containers for cooking rice. Lin says — and his customers agree — that they retain the aroma and flavor of cooked rice better than any modern pots, and are especially popular with sellers of steamed and glutinous rice. Lin also says there is nothing like a wooden bathtub for taking herbal baths.

People are often surprised that Lin insists on staying in business. He could easily lease his property and probably earn more from one month's rental than he does from an entire year of working in his shop. Lin says some contractors have even offered to put up a 12-story building on the site, promising him ownership of the first six floors which would guarantee him thousands of dollars a month in rents. But Lin has turned down all offers. "This is one of the only shops like this in Taiwan. It would be a pity if we closed and allowed this art to die out," he says without a hint of hesitation.

Lin Hwang-yi, Lin's one and only son shares that sentiment. He's now learning his father's craft and plans to keep the ancient art of cooperage alive in the family's old shop for at least a third generation.

Friends escape the pressures of modern life with a
relaxing cup of tea at a teahouse **(below)**. Though
not as elaborate as Japanese ceremonies, Chinese
still maintain that tea-making should have a certain
gongfu, or proper style.

Tea for You

For years teahouses in Taipei were small,
dingy-looking places where the elderly men of
the neighborhood or village went to relax over a pot
of tea, play a game of wei chei, and engage in small
talk with friends. All this began to change in the late
1970s, however, when a few shops opened up around
the city to cater to a new generation with a new-found
respect for the past.

Indeed, the burgeoning popularity of teahouses
represents a rekindling of interest in things Chinese
among Taipei's young people, a desire to balance the
increasing Westernization of society and to revive
traditional aspects of Chinese culture. More importantly, a teahouse is a place where people seeking to
escape the pressures of modern urban society and the
hustle and bustle of city life can find some peace and
space, even if only for a few hours, before heading
back out into the jampacked streets and sidewalks of
the 20th Century.

Taipei's teahouses come in a variety of shapes and
sizes. They range from Japanese style affairs to art
galleries to rustic farmhouses. Many utilize the
rejuvenated allure of culture to attract customers,
staging folk and artistic events and seminars on
calligraphy, paper-cutting, pottery, sculpture, traditional macrame and more.

Unfortunately, some establishments are not particularly lucrative, because their young owners are
seldom businessmen out to make a fortune. Most of
these entrepreneurs are more interested in providing
a congenial place for friends to meet and drink tea
while discussing the weighty issues of the day and
promoting cultural activities like art, film and drama.

A visitor to Taipei could not be blamed for
assuming that coffee is the national drink, since
coffee shops can be found on almost every street
corner. But China is where the art of tea drinking
originated. Only later was it assimilated by Japan,
where the tea ceremony is still a flourishing art.

By comparison, the Chinese method of making tea
is not as ritualized as Japan's tradition. The Chinese
approach the art of drinking tea as a release of
creativity and imagination and a way of enjoying
intimate friendship. The Chinese do not confine
people to a tea room nor does it force them to follow
rigid ceremony.

No one knows when tea drinking actually began
in China, but according to popular tradition Shen
Nung, a legendary emperor accidentally discovered
the brew when some leaves fell from a bush into
some drinking water he was boiling. Exhilirated by
its wonderful aroma and flavor, the emperor introduced the new drink to his subjects.

Historians say that tea was already being cultivated
around 350 AD Lu Yu's classic The Art of Drinking Tea was written during the 8th Century, when tea
was made from pressed cakes of tea leaves.

A visit to one of Taipei's tea shops will give you the
opportunity to enjoy drinking tea the way Chinese
connoisseurs do. However, as you will probably
have to manage all by yourself, a little advice is in
order. First, choose the variety of tea that you want to
sample from the many on the menu. Fill the empty
teapot with boiling water, then pour some hot water
into the cups to warm them. After that, dispose of the
contents of the pot and the cups.

Now put some tea leaves into the pot and fill it
again with boiling water. Tea is poured into the cups
this time, but is not to be drunk because the first brew
is considered too strong. Leave the tea leaves in the
pot, but empty the hot tea from the pot and cups into
the large bowl that is used to keep the teapot warm.

The pot is filled again with boiled water and the
leaves are left to soak for a few minutes. Tea is then
poured into the cups in succession, a little bit at a
time, until each cup is filled. This ensures that the
properties of the tea remain equal in each cup.
Before pouring the tea, however, the host should dry
the bottom of the teapot by running it around the rim
of the bowl in a counterclockwise direction, a
welcoming symbol.

Most teahouses serve more than just tea. Some
enhance the experience with side orders of such
favorite Chinese snacks as watermelon seeds,
peanuts, toasted squid, dried beancurd known as
tofu, rice cakes and preserved fruits.

As more and more people are finding out, in
Taipei there are few better ways to spend an evening
than huddled around a small table immersed in a pot
of tea and conversation with close friends.

The Chinese are ardent movie-goers who will sit through almost anything. Just about every box office hit from the United States eventually makes its way to Taipei, including a wide variety of the worst B-grade (perhaps more aptly D-grade) films with names like *"Bloodsuckers from Outer Space."* While some of the best films fall flat in Taipei, the worst sometimes turn out to be big hits. The Chinese also have a special place in their

heart for vintage classics. Crowds have been known to stand in long lines to get tickets for *Gone with the Wind* and other old favorites.

Taiwan also has its own thriving movie industry. Although it once had a well-deserved reputation for churning out low-quality films, great progress has been made in recent years. Some 83 Chinese-language movies were made in 1987 alone. The best of the new films realistically explore past and present problems in society, including subjects that were taboo until a few years ago.

Since almost all Chinese movies have English subtitles, it is possible and worthwhile for foreign visitors to spend a few hours watching

The steam rises from the hot sulfur spring in Hell's Valley, Peitou, just outside Taipei. Visitors enjoy eggs boiled in the hot mineral waters (above left and right). A sign (right) warns "hot enough to boil eggs, imagine what it can do to a person!"

some of the better locally-made films for some rare and extraordinary insights into the local culture. Among movies that have received critical acclaim are *Jade Love, Dust in the Wind, The Sandwich Man, The Boys of Fengkuei,* and *A Time to Live, A Time to Die.*

Hsimenting attracts large crowds of young people because the area is also littered with fast-food establishments and shops selling a wide variety of clothes, shoes and other merchandise. Some streets have been blocked off to traffic; in the square next to the Lai Lai department store, artists paint portraits and teenagers occasionally stage dance and music performances. Sundays are especially crowded and provide a good opportunity to literally rub elbows — not to mention most other parts of your body — with the Chinese.

Other than movie-going, eating and shopping probably rank as the top pastimes in Taipei and at the city's night markets, you can combine both. While there are a number of night markets of all sizes in Taipei, Hua Hsi Street, more exotically known as Snake Alley, has a carnival-like atmosphere that makes it the most colorful of the lot. And, as its name suggest, the adventurous can dine here on snake dishes prepared in several ways, most of them bloody and unappetizing. Visitors with weak stomachs may want to take a miss.

Operas also include a comic element, as shown by these clown types. Comic actors were popular on stage as they were always greeted by bursts of laughter. The patches of white and black around the actors' eyes, nose and mouth identify them as comedians or clowns.

Customers first select the juicy snake of their choice from small metal containers slithering with live specimens. Handlers then fish it out of the tank and hang it live on a wire. It is stretched out, then slit down the middle. The chef squeezes the blood and bile into a glass where it is mixed with herbs and *kaoliang*, a fiery brew made from wheat sorghum produced on the offshore island of Quemoy. The Chinese believe this tangy tonic is good for the eyes, lower spine, and, of course, provides a strong boost for male sexual vitality. The chef then cooks and serves the snake meat.

In addition to snake, a number of other small restaurants along the street serve somewhat more conventional dishes including live prawns, turtle, frog legs, squid and sausage. The competition for customers is quite stiff, however. One establishment specializing in

turtle meat, features a chimpanzee playing on a swing to lure the hungry.

Sandwiched in between the restaurants are bare-breasted body-builders and martial arts practitioners selling special health tonics. On Kuang Chow Street, which intersects Hua Hsi Street, peddlers set up several hundred carts and stands every evening to sell food, clothes, cassette tapes, tools, toys and just about anything else you can imagine.

The Nationalist government in Taiwan has always criticized mainland China's communist government for its failure to preserve Chinese culture and has prided itself for its own efforts in the area. In fact, many traditional customs

Scenes from a Taiwanese opera, performed in honor of a temple god (above and right). Opera troupes travel from area to area, performing on temporary stages. They often stage their performances in front of temples.

denounced by Beijing as nothing more than superstition are still practiced fervently today by the people of Taiwan. On April 5 each year, for example, families celebrate tomb sweeping day by cleaning and tidying up the graves of their ancestors, then offer meat, vegetable and wine sacrifices, and burn money for the spirits of the departed.

During the seventh month of the lunar calendar the gates of hell open and legions of hungry ghosts return to earth for their annual

sure that everything is done just right, in accordance with ancient custom. The costumes used are based on those worn during the Chou Dynasty (BC 1122-256) and, while the music scores only date back as far as the Ming Dynasty, the types of instruments played predate Confucius himself.

During the early migration from the mainland to Taiwan, the Chinese brought along their religious traditions and these have continued to grow throughout the island. Chinese

month-long visit; to keep them from causing trouble, the living lavish the ghosts with feasts of fish, pork, chicken and duck. Interestingly, an impromptu motorcycle-racing fad that gained popularity and attracted thousands of spectators during the hot summer nights of 1987 despite numerous accidents and deaths and the unsuccessful intervention of the police ended abruptly when ghost month arrived. The drivers suddenly seemed to lose all their nerve and cool.

The Chinese love festivals and it is no exaggeration to say that you can observe some kind of age-old festival in Taipei every month. The ceremony celebrating the birth of Confucius (BC 551-479) is just one example. Every year on September 28, the Confucius Temple in Taipei is crowded with people before daybreak when the complicated ceremony begins. Great pains are taken to make

religion in Taiwan can be described as a combination of folk belief, Taoism, and Buddhism, all rolled into one. In fact, many Chinese don't make a sharp distinction between Taoism and Buddhism.

The Lungshan Temple, for example, originally started out as a Buddhist temple dedicated to the Goddess of Mercy. Over the years, though, a number of Taoist gods managed to sneak their way in. When the Japanese ruled Taiwan, they tried to stamp out anything that was even vaguely Chinese. Since many of the gods and goddesses in Taoism are derived from historical heroes, such as Kuan Kung, who does double-duty as the God of War and

Costumes, make-up and gestures signal different types of opera characters. One actress (left) plays a hua tan, a mischievious and flirtatious maiden. Her coy eye movements are considered attractive. Wu tan roles (above) demand acrobatic skills.

the God of Business, the Japanese ordered all temples shut down. The temple members responded by removing all the Taoist gods from the main altar, but built a separate altar in the rear for them. Thus, if you visit the back of the Lungshan Temple today, you will find Kuan Kung, Matsu, goddess of the sea, and other Taoist deities.

Kuan Yin, one of Taiwan's most popular patrons, is actually claimed by Taoists and

Buddhists alike. Her image is found in most temples around the island. Kuan Yin is often portrayed standing or sitting in a lotus; in yet another display of her pervasive influence one holy card distributed by the Catholic Church in Taiwan years ago portrayed a Chinese-looking Blessed Mother standing in a lotus.

Religion still plays a major part in the daily lives of the people of Taipei. On special religious holidays businessmen set up small tables in front of their shops, piled high with food offerings. They also burn "gold" paper money, as offerings to the gods. And many taxi drivers have little red Buddhist medallions hanging from their rearview mirrors, much the

Taipei is developing its own sense of style and glamor. Many Taipei trends are set by TV and film stars like Chen Hsiu-chen, signing autographs for anxious fans (right). The dress of these two mo deng (modern) girls (above) shows a Japanese influence.

way Catholics in the United States once pinned St. Christopher medals to the dashboards of their cars.

Statues of any number of Chinese gods can be seen at any number of temples around the city. Their courtyards and halls are packed with worshipers on holidays and the air thick with the intoxicating smells of burning incense. When people need advice, they stand in front of the altar dropping kidney-shaped divining blocks, usually asking the gods' opinion about love or business. There are many people who would not think of entering into marriage or a new business without first consulting the gods.

Another religious relic, ancestor worship, also remains an integral part of life in Taiwan; many families in Taipei still keep an ancestral altar in a conspicuous corner of their modern high-rise apartments. The altars vary in shape from small racks on the wall to large, elaborately-carved redwood tables and family members place food offerings on them twice a month. The only concession to modern times is that on many family altars, as well as in the temples, tins of fancy imported cookies and crackers now stand next to the time-honored offerings of chicken, fish, pork and fruit.

The art of *fengshui*, or geomancy, has also survived the centuries. It is used to determine the proper position of buildings and tombs and can bring bad luck when done incorrectly. One coffee shop in Taipei had its front door torn down three times and shifted to different sides of the store because the owner felt that bad *fengshui* was responsible for his lack of business. He eventually sold the store; the new owner immediately moved the door back to its original spot.

Another holdover from the past are Taipei's dwindling legion of street vendors. Hundreds of years ago these itinerant entrepreneurs were a common sight in China. They moved from town to town and street to street shouting out the names of their wares. While some of Taipei's burgeoning corps of young urban professionals see this type of business as a nuisance and the police try to keep it off certain streets, many people in Taipei still find these roving vendors an inexpensive and convenient way to shop.

Peddlers in Taipei today fall into two categories. The first is composed of relatively stationary types who set up their tables on sidewalks in busy areas of the city and sell a wide variety of goods. The second category covers the more traditional traveling vendor who peddles or pushes his cart through the small streets of the older neighborhoods.

In the mornings, housewives who have not had an opportunity to go to the market, rush out as soon as they hear the call of the vegetable man: *"Buay cai oh, buay cai oh!"* Later in the morning, children scamper out of their homes carrying bowls for a delightful dollop of *douhua*, a gelatin-like beancurd mixed with peanuts, sugar and ginger. The window-screen repairman carries all his tools and supplies on his tiny cart and the seller of

mount tape recorders on their carts. Obviously that saves a lot of energy, not to mention breath, but the amplified sounds just don't have quite the same old aura. Worse than that, as the city's buildings get taller and taller, roving peddlers are rapidly becoming an endangered species. It's hard to be heard 12 flights above the roar of the city, even with a tape recorder.

One common saying in Taiwan has it that

household goods is a veritable store on wheels, a mountain of bamboo poles, brooms, mops and buckets that's so high it dwarfs both the driver and his cart.

Some of the vendors make a distinctive sound that is easily-recognized by the people in the neighborhood. No one who has ever heard the mournful wail *"shui ba zang,"* on cold winter nights can ever forget it.

Soi ba dzang, as this Taiwanese expression is spelled, is hot sticky rice cooked in banana leaves. And it wasn't too long ago that the blind masseuse still walked through the streets playing his flute to get attention.

Now many of these mobile merchants

Food is one of the most integral ingredients in Chinese culture. Master chefs in Taipei create incomparable dishes like this delectable dragon, fashioned from shrimp and carved carrots (above).

the three best things in life are an American house, a Japanese wife and Chinese food. Without a doubt, one of Taipei's best-preserved traditions is the art of Chinese cooking. There's inarguably no other place in the world where you can sample so many different kinds of Chinese cuisine in such a small area. In addition to the cuisines of Hunan, Sichuan and Canton, which can be easily found in any major city around the world, visitors to Taipei can also sample the specialties of Hubei, Shanxi, and Mongolia, as well as local Taiwanese and Hakka dishes.

The reason for this is simple. When Generalissimo Chiang Kai-shek began his retreat from the mainland in the 1940s, some two million mainlanders from every corner of China migrated to Taiwan. Many of these people settled down in Taipei and opened restaurants specializing in the dishes of their home provinces, thereby preserving one of the best traditions China has to offer.

All in all, the most remarkable thing about Taipei is its people. They are hardworking and disciplined, characteristics reflected in the city's rapid progress in recent years. They are also extremely outgoing, friendly and generous. If you stand on the sidewalk looking bewildered and foreign, someone is bound to eventually offer directions, or even guide you

deftly maneuvers between buses, his four passengers hanging on for dear life.

Some say the Chinese have a different sense of space and a ride on a Taipei bus seems to bear that out. No matter how crowded or uncomfortable the buses may be, no one loses their cool. In the past, there was no concept of privacy. That may be changing now as the practice of an extended family — grandparents, parents, children, grandchildren all liv-

to any destination in which you express interest.

Most Taipei residents follow the Chinese tradition of rising early. At the crack of dawn, they can be seen in almost any park in the city, practicing martial arts, the Chinese form of shadow boxing known as *taichichuan*, learning the waltz, tango, or modern dance, or just playing a game of badminton. Before heading off to work or school people stop by little breakfast shops and stands for a hot bowl of soybean milk and baked bread wrapped around a cruller-like stick of deep-fried dough.

Each morning, cars, buses and motorcycles jam Taipei's streets as people head off to work and school. Whole families wedge themselves atop a motorcycle; father drops off mother at work and the children at either the nursery or school. It is not uncommon to see a mother with an infant tied to her back with one child in front of her and one in front of the father as he

ing under the same roof — fades into the past. But essentially, the Chinese, like the Japanese, remain a group people. They enjoy doing things together and feel more comfortable in large numbers.

Contrary to popular belief, however, the Chinese are not in the least bit patient when they are in such groups. Just stand in line at the post office or bank. Someone is bound to walk directly to the front of the line and shove his money past yours. Still, the Chinese never complain when this occurs. They may be more courteous in the presence of foreign visitors, but should someone sponge in front of you in a queue feel free to sponge back.

The presentation of Chinese food is as crucial as its preparation. The chefs of Taipei are artists in their own right. Not only do they produce tastes that titillate the palate, but they design food dishes that excite the eye (above).

Fix It with Fengshui

When Hang Pao-te, a respected architect, returned home to Taipei from studying at Princeton and Harvard in the 1960s, his first job was to design a house for a relative who was a high-ranking government official. But just when the official was about to move in, colleagues criticized the completed house as unfit; the fengshui, they said, was bad. To his embarrassment, the young architect was forced to invite a fengshui man, who didn't have the benefit of an Ivy League education, to look at his design and correct his "mistakes."

"That was when I realized the power of fengshui, Han recalls. "I began to study it right away."

Fengshui, which literally means "wind and water," is the ancient Chinese art of geomancy. It's based on the belief that inanimate objects can affect one's life. Thus, people in Taiwan and other Chinese communities still use fengshui today to determine the positioning of graves, houses and other buildings, including office towers, and furniture and office layouts.

Architects and interior decorators have learned, often the hard way, that the practice should not be taken lightly. After working long hours on their design blueprints, more than a few have been sent back to the drawing board after their designs were torn apart by their client's fengshui man.

When modern highrises go up in Taipei, the builder routinely calls in a geomancer, whether or not he believes in fengshui; he's well aware that a prospective occupant will call in their own geomancers to determine whether the building has the right fengshui to help rather than hinder his business. Some construction companies have even hired fengshui consultants as advisers.

Despite the fact that modernization has overtaken Taiwan, the geomancy business has boomed in recent years. Taipei alone has an estimated 10,000 practitioners. Local psychologists say the pressures and rapid change of modern society induce people to turn to traditional practices like fortune-telling and geomancy for comfort and a sense of their roots.

Geomancers follow old guidelines, some of which have some basis in common sense, in making their design recommendations. Raised ground, for instance, is considered a good place to build a building; that stands to reason, particularly in flood-prone cities. And when designing a house, geomancers generally recommend that its important area should be centrally located: that helps promote a close family unit. Mirrors with eight diagrams painted on them are commonly seen hanging over doors, because people believe, of course, that they deflect bad luck from a dwelling.

The color of a building can also come into play. Although most cultures consider fire-engine red loud and garish, it is common in Chinese communities, especially during important holidays, because it is the color of joy and festivity. Yellow was favored by ancient Chinese royalty, so it also enjoys popularity. Green is another auspicious shade, because of its connection with the earth, plants and fertility.

Real estate advertisements in newspapers frequently push "good fenghsui" as a selling point and it is common for builders, developers and clients alike to move their doors from one location to another in an attempt to improve the fengshui. Special rulers are also sold for measuring the size of a family altar and the distance between the gods placed on them. If everything is not just right, a family or proprietor could be in for a spell of bad luck. One geomancer says that the removal of even a single misplaced nail can end problems.

Fengshui is taken seriously by all segments of Taiwan's society from small village farmers right up to corporate decision-makers. When the Evergreen Group put up its new headquarters in Taipei in 1987, it erected a large white ship's mast in a small garden adjoining the building. Unfortunately, the mast was directly opposite the door of the Cathay Construction

Company just acros the street. Cathay officials complained that the mast was like a dagger pointed at their offices, was thus ruining their fengshui *and demanded that it be moved. Evergreen balked, saying they had no other place to put it. The dispute simmered and wasn't resolved until Cathay moved into a new office building.*

One well-known government official who suffered a political setback years ago was advised by his geomancer to move his front door. It faced oncoming traffic, "a spear aimed at the office." The man moved his door to the side of the building. Shortly afterwards, he was appointed to a senior post in the nation's government.

Nevertheless, geomancy is not the foolproof cureall it's often purported to be. In the early 1980s, when foreign banks in Taipei were experiencing a string of bad loans, the American general manager of one bank called in a geomancer. Although the bank followed the geomancer's advice by rearranging the offices of the general manager and personnel manager, the bank led that year in the number of bad loans that it had to write off.

Han says that modern-day geomancy is arbitrary, has numerous interpretations, and that it is not uncommon for several geomancers all to come up with totally different conclusions. In fact, fengshui *was originally used only to determine the position of burial sites and did not include buildings or furniture until recent times.*

Han does not believe in fengshui, *which he describes as a proto-science. But he says that a knowledge of it can produce a better understanding of Chinese culture. "If you don't understand fengshui, you will still understand Chinese architecture, but you will miss a lot," he says. "Now when I look at the traditional Chinese environment, I understand it better."*

Indeed, present-day attitudes toward fengshui *in modern Taipei can be summed up in the words of Chi Kang (AD 223-262), one of the Seven Worthies of the Bamboo Grove. "I'm hesitant to make a hard and fast judgment. I wouldn't want to say that divination can tell your future, but I wouldn't want to say there are no unlucky houses either." In short, it's probably safer to believe in* fengshui, *than not to.*

Perhaps the most exciting time of day in Taipei is after dark. Blinding banks of gaudy neon signs crammed with Chinese characters light up the place. People crowd the stores as they stop to shop on their way home from work. Vendors busy themselves at their street stalls, whipping up Chinese-style fast food for those too busy to sit down and eat.

The Chung Shan North Road area abounds with nightlife; thousands of bars and clubs in the district switch on the alluring technicolor sign after the sunsets. On the conventional side, Japanese-style *karaoke* clubs, where patrons can get up and sing to their heart's content accompanied by tape recorded music, are also exceedingly popular.

On the wild side, Taipei may be one of the few places in the world where barber shops are part of the nightlife. Inarguably, Taipei has more barber shops per acre than any other city

in Asia, and some of them may have more lighted, candy-striped barber poles per square inch swirling out front than any other tonsorial establishment in the world. These barber shops are not quite what they seem, however; few specialize in cutting heads of hair. Most are nothing more than thinly-veiled fronts for massage parlors that offer an astonishing variety of sexual entertainment.

If your proclivities do not lean in that direction, a coffee shop may be more your cup of tea. In Taipei, the coffee shop is almost as institutionalized as the barberless barber shop. It's a place where you can order an entire meal or just meditate for hours over an expensive

*The new program of singers at a West Gate music hall is displayed (**left**) to attract patrons. The chart (**above**) is used by fortune tellers to foresee the future in people's features, or should we say to foresee the features of peoples' futures?*

Songbird descending from the ceiling: *singers like this woman (**above**) in a tight-fitting sequined* chi-pao *have long been the main attraction at Taipei's many nightclubs. The floorshow (**above and below left**) is a brightly-costumed extravaganza of Western and Chinese influences.*

cuppa. Bear in mind that the steep prices include an unlimited claim on your seat. No one cares how long you stay. Students while away hours over a single sip while studying, other young people chat with friends and businessmen come to clinch deals.

Despite a curfew that requires most businesses to shut down by 1 a.m., many establishments — from bars to corner noodle stands — stay open until the wee hours,

closing shop just as their fellow citizens are heading to the parks for their early morning exercise. You may have to tap on the closed door or shuttered window of a bar to get in, however.

As modernization sweeps over Taipei bringing ever-increasing waves of western influence, more and more Chinese, young and old, have begun feeling a growing desire to retain, and in some cases, revive, something of their heritage. In recent years, the rekindling of interest in Chinese culture that has sprouted in the city can be seen in such simple things as tea shops, clothes and the city's new buildings.

Numerous tea shops have opened serving a

A martial arts expert leaps in the air and throws a flying side kick (right). Martial arts continue to be popular, but other forms of physical development are practiced too, as seen by the bulk and muscle definition of this oiled-up bodybuilder (above).

variety of China's favorite drink and simple snacks. They have proven to be especially popular with students, artists and intellectuals. Some come wearing the creations of local designers who have incorporated traditional Chinese tailoring concepts in women's skirts and suits. These fashions are not only modern and functional, but also include some Chinese flavor and flare.

Architects are also beginning to follow suit, although it's proving more difficult because no one is really able to really define just what modern Chinese architecture is. When the island's economy first began taking off Western post-modern buildings with miniature steeples and sloping roofs started sprouting up all over the city. In recent years, the trend has shifted towards red-tiled roofs, circular windows and Chinese brick work. The dilemma of creating something that is both modern and

Chinese is shared by writers, artist, dancers and musicians. All are struggling to find their own identity in a city that is still searching for itself. Architect Lee Chian-lang has said that it will be another 20 years before local architects have the confidence to design something that is truly original. That prognosis may apply to those in other fields as well.

Essentially, Taipei is in a period of transition, much like the one Japan experienced after World War II. A lot of experimentation is going on and, although not everyone is satisfied with the results thus far, it is nevertheless an exciting phase in the development of the city. The pervading feeling is one of optimism.

Children astride a prancing bronze horse in Taipei's New Park (**right**). *The horse has been a popular subject in Chinese art for centuries. Students sit on motor scooters (**above**), one of Taipei's most common forms of transportation.*

These Elementary School students, *their names embroidered on their uniform shirts, carry pictures of Dr Sun Yat-sen, the father of Modern China. Dr Sun was a medical doctor who traveled around the world gathering support for the anti-Manchu movement, which freed China from the Ching Dynasty.*

Back of the Book

This section provides a handy, compact package of exciting insights, entertaining tidbits, and invaluable tips that will help enhance your trip to Taipei. The main maps depict Taipei's location on the island of Taiwan, the island's location in the region, and a detailed look at metropolitan Taipei. Little-known facts about the city in Taipei Trivia reveal why there is no front gate in the Confucian Temple and why lovers should avoid the Chihnan Temple. There's also a section of suggested Tours of the city and its surrounding that includes detailed maps of the areas covered, followed by a look at some interesting sights that are Off the Beaten Track. Best Bets lists the best places in Taipei to experience acupuncture, buy books and watch a Chinese Opera, among other recommendations. Finally, the Travel Notes summarize basic information needed to get you to and through Taipei and back.

A 25-ton bronze statue of Generalissimo Chiang Kai-shek (left) smiles down benevolently upon visitors on the main floor of the Chung-cheng Memorial Hall. Overhead is the white and blue symbol of the Republic of China, set within an intricately carved wooden ceiling.

Night is the most magical time of day *in Taipei, when the city awakens with the lights of myriad neon signs and the sounds of people enjoying life. In this view of the metropolitan area, looking out from the Grand Hotel, the silent bulk of the new Taipei Fine Arts Museum stands in the foreground.*

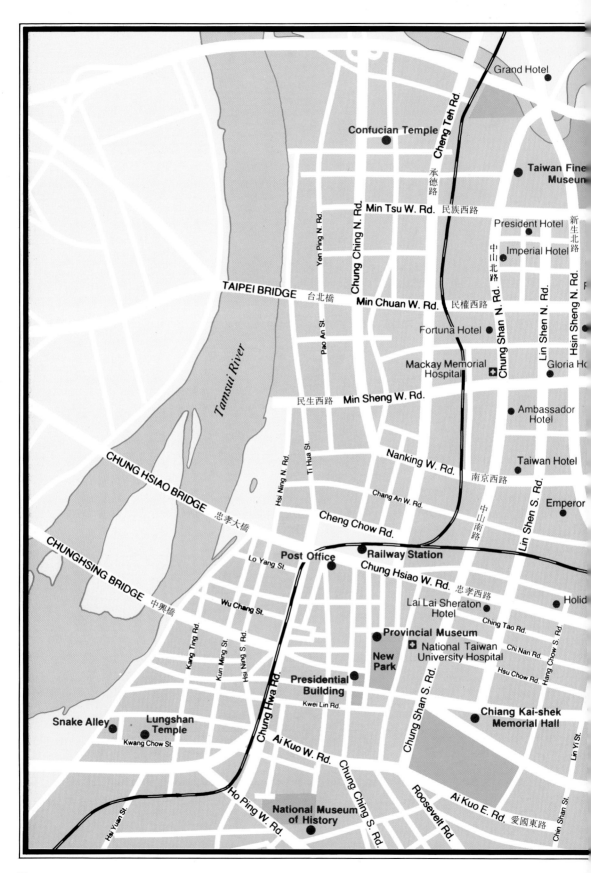

Grand Hotel

Confucian Temple 孔子廟

Cheng Teh Rd

承德路

Taiwan Fine
Museum

Min Tsu W. Rd. 民族西路

President Hotel

新生北路

Yen Ping N. Rd.

Chung Ching N. Rd.

中山北路

Imperial Hotel

TAIPEI BRIDGE 台北橋

Min Chuan W. Rd. 民權西路

Chung Shan N. Rd.

Lin Shen N. Rd.

Hsin Sheng N. Rd.

Pao An St.

Fortuna Hotel

Tamsui River

Mackay Memorial
Hospital

Gloria Ho

民生西路 Min Sheng W. Rd.

Ambassador
Hotel

Hsi Ning N. Rd.

Ti Hua St.

Nanking W. Rd.

南京西路

Taiwan Hotel

CHUNG HSIAO BRIDGE 忠孝大橋

Chang An W. Rd.

中山南路

Emperor

Lin Shen S. Rd.

Cheng Chow Rd.

CHUNGHSING BRIDGE 中興橋

Lo Yang St.

Post Office

Railway Station

Chung Hsiao W. Rd. 忠孝西路

Holid

Wu Chang St.

Lai Lai Sheraton
Hotel

Ching Tao Rd.

Hang Chow S. Rd.

Chi Nan Rd.

Kang Ting Rd.

Kun Ming St.

Hsi Ning S. Rd.

Provincial Museum

New
Park

National Taiwan
University Hospital

Hsu Chow Rd.

Chung Hwa Rd.

Presidential
Building

Chung Shan S. Rd.

Chiang Kai-shek
Memorial Hall

Kwei Lin Rd.

Snake Alley

Lungshan
Temple

Lin Yi St.

Kwang Chow St.

Ai Kuo W. Rd.

Chung Ching S. Rd.

Roosevelt Rd.

Ai Kuo E. Rd. 愛國東路

Chin Shan St.

Hsi Yuan St.

Ho Ping W. Rd.

National Museum
of History

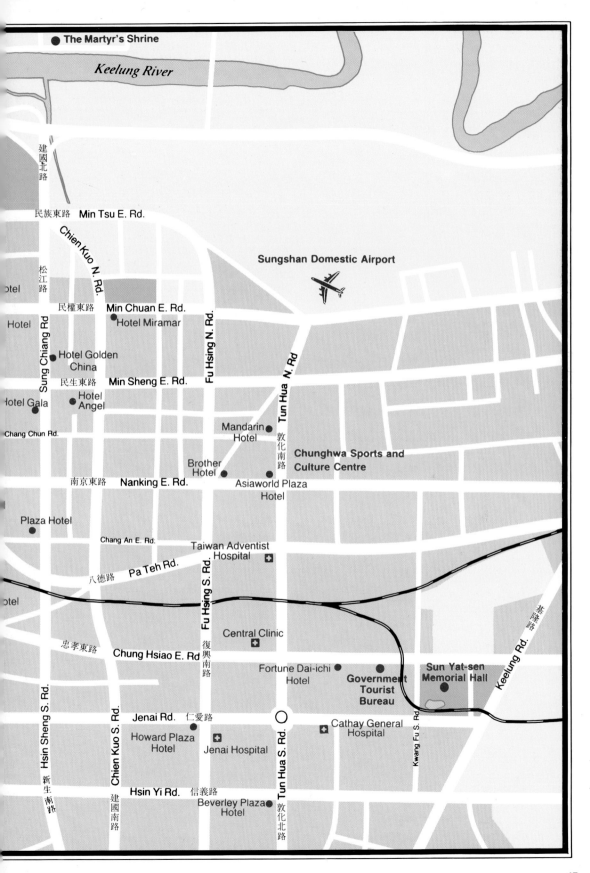

The Martyr's Shrine

Keelung River

建國北路

民族東路 Min Tsu E. Rd.

Chien Kuo N. Rd.

松江路

Sungshan Domestic Airport

Hotel

民權東路 Min Chuan E. Rd.

Hotel Miramar

Hotel

Sung Chiang Rd

Fu Hsing N. Rd.

Hotel Golden China

民生東路 Min Sheng E. Rd.

Tun Hua N. Rd

Hotel Gala

Hotel Angel

Chang Chun Rd.

Mandarin Hotel

敦化南路

Chunghwa Sports and Culture Centre

Brother Hotel

南京東路 Nanking E. Rd.

Asiaworld Plaza Hotel

Plaza Hotel

Chang An E. Rd.

Taiwan Adventist Hospital

八德路 Pa Teh Rd.

Fu Hsing S. Rd.

Hotel

Central Clinic

忠孝東路 Chung Hsiao E. Rd

復興南路

Fortune Dai-ichi Hotel

Government Tourist Bureau

Sun Yat-sen Memorial Hall

基隆路 Keelung Rd.

Hsin Sheng S. Rd.

Chien Kuo S. Rd.

Jenai Rd. 仁愛路

Howard Plaza Hotel

Jenai Hospital

Tun Hua S. Rd.

Cathay General Hospital

Kwang Fu S. Rd.

新生南路

建國南路

Hsin Yi Rd. 信義路

Beverley Plaza Hotel

敦化北路

Taipei Trivia

SIDE ENTRANCE ONLY. According to Chinese custom, only a *Chang Yuan*, the most successful candidate in the imperial examination, was allowed to enter the Confucian Temple through the front gate. Since Taipei did not have a *Chang Yuan* prior to the establishment of the Republic of China in 1911 when the examination system was abolished, the Confucian Temple in the city was not permitted to build a front gate.

GETTING TALLER. In 1973 the 20-story Taipei Hilton was the capital's tallest building. Today it is dwarfed by dozens of buildings that have gone up in recent years.

CHOP-CHOP. Chinese name chops have been used as the traditional form of signature for thousands of years. Today, the Chinese in Taiwan still use their individual name chops to finalize contracts, sign documents, cash checks, and other purposes. It is said that no two chops are alike and that it is more difficult to forge a chop than a signature. A person who loses his chop must publish a notice in local newspapers to automatically make the chop invalid.

THE GODS MUST BE JEALOUS. Local legend says unmarried lovers should not visit the Chihnan temple in the Taipei suburb of Mucha. Lu Tong-ping, the main god of the temple and one of the Eight Immortals, once failed in love and is said to get extremely jealous when he sees couples together at the temple. The legend has it that Lu uses his supernatural powers to drive the lovers apart. Many Chinese tales recount Lu's many successful sexual encounters with beautiful maidens and goddesses.

PROPHETIC DREAMS. The Chihnan Temple has a special room beside the main altar for those who want to experience "prophetic dreams." To do so, a guest must eat only vegetarian food for three days prior to dreamtime to make sure he is physically and spiritually clean. Then on the appointed evening, he must kowtow at the altar, burn incense and tell the god Lu Tong-ping his problem. The dreamer then goes to the room to sleep and wait for a dreamy communication from Lu. After each dream the guest throws crescent-shaped divining blocks that indicate if the dream is the correct one.

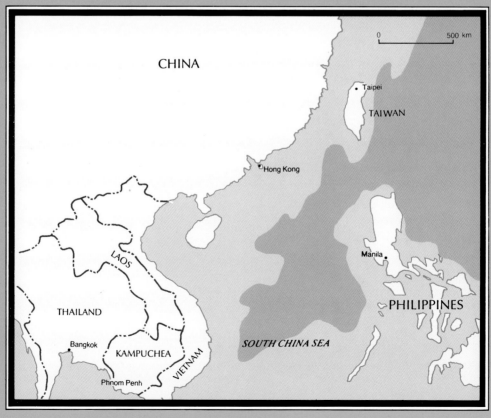

HONORABLE FOREIGNERS. Roosevelt Road, named after American President Franklin Delano Roosevelt, is the only street in Taipei named after a foreigner. Taipei's New Park has what is believed to be the only non-religious statue on the island dedicated to a foreigner. A bust of General Clair Chennault, who resigned from the U.S. Army in 1937 and went to China to organize air defenses for Chiang Kai-shek in his battle against the Japanese, stands in the rear of the park alongside a monument to Chennault's Flying Tigers.

SEEING RED. After the Nationalist government retreated to Taiwan in 1949 following its defeat at the hands of the Chinese communists, it attempted to wipe out all reminders of its foe. In fact, the hotel rating system utilizes plum blossoms instead of stars which are a prominent feature of the flag of the People's Republic of China. Thus, there are no five-star hotels in Taipei, but there are some five-plum blossom establishments. Furthermore, there is no Route Eight bus because of the government's hatred of the Communist Eighth Route Army.

EVERYBODY'S HAPPY. Well, at least everybody who wins *Everybody's Happy* is happy. *Tachialo*, an illegal numbers game which began in central Taiwan in 1985 and literally translates as "everybody's happy" in English, has snaked its way around the entire island in just two years, affecting life in the capital in ways no one could have imagined. Despite its name, the game has been blamed for a spate of bankruptcies, divorces, insanity, suicides and murders. For every story of a person who became a millionaire overnight after hitting a winning number, there are dozens of other tales about people who have suffered from their fanatical fascination with the game.

Organized around a well-known and respected member of the local community entrusted with bets known as a "head," the winning number is determined by the government's Liberty Lottery in which gamblers pick any two numbers from 00 to 99. Preoccupation with the game has reached such a fever pitch that *Tachialo* has almost become a national pastime. Factory workers in many areas don't show up for work on the day of the drawing forcing some companies to redo production schedules. In an attempt to cope with the problem, other concerns have resorted to sponsoring the underground lotteries themselves just to keep their employees on the premises. Some retired soldiers have lost their life savings and education authorities have admitted that junior high school students are participating. Even prison inmates are playing the game from behind bars.

On drawing days, players overload telephone lines with last minute bets and requests for winning numbers. All this has also affected the financial system. The Central Bank reports that the lottery days are the busiest for local banks, with withdrawals totaling as much as US$400 million around the island. Authorities estimate that capital invested in the illegal lottery accounts for about five per cent of the nation's total circulating currency in 1987. As for the stock market, "heads" pour their temporary, but large, holdings into securities to try to turn a quick profit before making payoffs.

With so much at stake, *Tachialo* players resort to any means of coming up with a winning number. In one ghoulish incident when a bus plunged 60 meters off the side of Taipei's Yangming Mountain killing 22 people, crowds rushed to the scene for a look at the last two numbers on the license plate. Scientific-minded players turn to computers, while the more traditional Chinese put their trust in the gods, ghosts and ancestors. As a result, geomancers, fortune-tellers and Taoist monks are the game's only sure winners. Bettors flock to their doors for assistance in picking the lucky number. This has in turn created a shortage of mediums, prompting the opening of a rash of schools that can train more.

One of the favorite haunts of bettors the night before a drawing are graveyards. Night markets peddling food and drink to thousands spring up around Taipei's cemeteries on such occasions. Armed with flashlights and magnifying glasses, the crowds search for signs, usually written in the earth, that may indicate a winning number. And cars have been seen backed up for an entire kilometer along a road in Pali Village in Taipei County, as anxious gamblers waited for a lucky number in front of a Dutch general's tomb.

Temples are another popular place to seek

numbers, but the players, aware that it may be a bit sacrilegious to ask respectable gods for such help, have turned to lesser gods in the Chinese pantheon. The Monkey King and his sidekick, Pigsy, famous characters from the Chinese classic, *Journey to the West*, are just two examples. In fact, these lowly gods have enjoyed a resurgence in popularity in recent years, as winners' donations are used to carry out the renovation of old temples and construction of new ones dedicated in their honor. Gods who come up with winning numbers earn such rewards as gold chains hung around the necks of their statues, big feasts and even an occasional striptease show from grateful female winners.

On the other hand, losers have been known to vent their anger on gods who fail to come up with a winning combination. Consequently, some temples have had to hire security guards to prevent the statues of their deities from being manhandled.

GOING TO THE DOGS. Taipei County has what may be the only temple dedicated to a dog. The Temple of 18 Princes, along the coast just one hour outside Taipei, is the burial place of a dog and 17 sailors who perished together in a shipwreck 200 years ago. The temple is popular with taxi drivers, underworld figures, bar girls and gamblers, who believe the dog has special powers. They drive out to the temple late at night and place cigarette butts, instead of incense sticks, on nails in front of a granite statue of the dog that marks its grave. Worshipers buy a piece of red cloth which they use to rub the statue's head. These red cloths, miniature statues and medallions with the dog's picture are frequently found in Taipei taxi cabs.

GHOST OF A WEDDING. If a young person in Taiwan dies before getting married the deceased's family will sometimes arrange a posthumous wedding for the departed son or daughter — with a living person. Several years ago in Taipei a taxi driver agreed to marry the ghost of a young girl that he had struck and killed accidentally with his car.

FINDING LOST HORIZONS. A knowledge of mainland China's geography will prove helpful in getting around Taipei's bewildering maze of streets. Most streets are named after towns, cities, rivers, mountains and other features on the mainland and their location roughly corresponds to the actual place on the map of China. The three main streets that run east and west are named after Dr. Sun Yat-sen's ideological program, *San Min Chui*, the Three Principles of the People: *Min Sheng* (the people's livelihood), *Min Chuan* (the people's rights or democracy) and *Min Tsu* (nationalism).

UNLUCKY NUMBER. Szu, the Chinese word for the number "four," has the same sound as the word for "die." That's the reason why so many buildings and hospitals in Taipei do not have a 4th floor, much like many buildings in the West's eliminate the 13th floor. And there are no Number 4 buses.

POINTING THE WRONG WAY. Contrary to its name, the North Gate, which dates from the Ching Dynasty, does not face due north. According to Chinese custom, forts must be layed out in accordance with the principles of geomancy which dictate that it be situated several degrees to the east.

CROWDED. Hsui Land Primary School is the largest elementary school in Taiwan and, possibly, the world. Some 12,000 students and 300 teachers, an average of 60 per class, jam the popular school. Furthermore, an average of one full class of students transfers there from other Taipei schools each month.

CASTING FATE TO THE WIND. The winding road from Taipei to Ilan is fraught with danger. Accidents and fatalities occur there frequently. In order to appease the spirits of those who lost their lives there (probably while trying to pass on a curve) people starting out in either direction throw paper money out the window before setting out, and then often try to pass on curves anyhow. Buddhist inscriptions can also be found along the highway.

BETELMANIA. You may notice a red substance on the streets of Taipei that looks like blood. It's more likely betel, also known as Chinese chewing gum. Betel is a chewing substance popular in many parts of Asia since ancient time. It comes from a nut and contains a narcotic stimulant. The seeds of the betel nut and other flavorings are smeared onto a betel pepper leaf which is then rolled into a ball and chewed. Small stands selling betel can be found all over Taiwan. Some are open 24 hours and use giant replicas of a betel nut hanging overhead to attract customers. The hazards of betel include the fact that users spit its blood red liquid in almost any convenient place, staining the spot. Many users develop permanently stained teeth.

CHINESE ROBIN HOOD. The Liao Tien-ting Temple near Tamsui is named after a robber known as the Robin Hood of Taipei. Like the popular hero of Western legend, Liao stole from the rich to give to the poor. His temple is said to be a popular place of worship for local thieves. Ironically some of them have been nabbed there by alert police.

HAVE YOUR BOWL AND EAT IT TOO. A Taipei inventor has developed a rice bowl — made of rice. He pours uncooked rice and water into a mold, then presses them for a few seconds with a heated steel ball. The bowls, which can hold hot water for several minutes, conveniently can be eaten afterwards as a snack. They are also sold to farmers for animal feed or thrown into the river for the fish to eat. The inventor hopes his product will not only help reduce the island's rice surplus, but cut down pollution caused by the disposal of styrofoam bowls.

Taipei Tours

DOWNTOWN WALKING TOUR. Although the center of commercial activity in Taipei has shifted in recent years, a number of historical buildings and government offices remain in the old downtown area. Most of the buildings constructed during the early years of the Japanese Occupation (1895-1945) are European-style, a form popular in Japan around the turn of the century.

Begin your stroll at the **Taipei City Hall (1)** , 39 Chang An W. Rd. This structure was originally built in 1920 by the Japanese as an elementary school for their children. There are several traditional shops in the area, most notably the **Lin Tien Cooperage (2)**, one of the few remaining bucketmakers in Taiwan (see "Hooked on Wood".)

In 1913 Dr. Sun Yat Sen, the father of the Republic of China, was on his way to Japan and stopped over in Taiwan. The Japanese-style **Wu Mei Hotel (3)**, where Dr. Sun stayed at the time, has been reconstructed on the site with a surrounding garden and a small pavilion and pond.

The Control Yuan (4), the nation's highest supervisory body, was built in 1915 to serve as an administrative headquarters for the ruling Japanese. The large dome, surrounded by smaller domes, appears to be of either Byzantine or Eastern European style. Fortunately, when a wing was added to the building in 1987, designers utilized the original materials and style, using the same red brick with gray trim and circular windows.

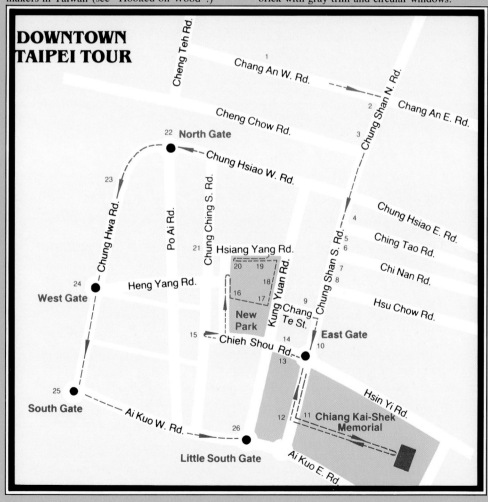

DOWNTOWN TAIPEI TOUR

The **Parliament Building (5)** was also a school during the Occupation. The **Chinan Presbyterian Church (6)** was built in 1916 for the use of professors teaching at the National Taiwan University Hospital and Medical School. Next to the **Ministry of Education (7)** is the **Chinese Handicraft Mart (8)**, a government-sponsored store that sells a wide variety of Chinese handicrafts.

National Taiwan University Hospital (9) was built by Kondo Julo, a Japanese architect who specialized in hospital architecture. Note the building's Ionic columns on the second level and the pediment on the top level. The huge lobby with its high curved glass ceiling and rows of archways is very impressive and also worth a look.

Serving as the traffic circle here is the **East Gate (10)**. The old city wall originally ran along the street here connecting this gate with the other city gates, and the inside area was known as "Old Taipei."

The imposing **Chiang Kai-shek Memorial Hall (11)**, completed in 1980, has a museum on the ground floor with displays of photographs and personal items belonging to the late Generalissimo, who established Taiwan's Chinese Nationalist government. The honor guard on the main floor changes every hour on the hour.

Opposite the Memorial Hall is the **National Central Library (12)**, which was opened in 1986. It houses some 12,000 rare Chinese books, including more than 600 Sung and Yuan Dynasty imprint titles, ancient stone rubbings, Tunhuang scrolls and wooden and bamboo tablets inscribed during the Han Dynasty. Next door to the library is the **Ministry of Foreign Affairs (13)**.

The **Taipei Guest House (14)**, completed in 1912, has a high wall around it and is only partially visible from the street. This French renaissance-style building is considered one of the best examples of Japanese workmanship. It was originally the residence of the Japanese governor-general, but the Ministry of Foreign Affairs laid claim to the building after Japan's surrender and turned it into a posh lodging for visiting VIPs. A garden and lagoon enhance the grounds of the mansion.

The **Presidential Building (15)** took seven years to complete. The Japanese opened it in 1919 as their governor-general's residence. At that time, its 660-meter high central tower made it the tallest building in Taipei. During the Japanese Occupation, the building was looked upon as a symbol of the authority of the colonial rulers. During World War II, allied bombs damaged the renaissance-style building, but it was renovated after the end of the war.

Smack in the middle of the downtown area lies **Taipei New Park**. Enter through the gate that faces Heng Yang Road and bear right around the outdoor theater. On the far side, you will find the **Chi Kung Hao Yi Arch (16)**. It was erected in 1888 during the Ching Dynasty near the intersection of Hsiang Yang Road and Chung Ching South Road and moved to its present location in 1905.

On the east side of the park is a large **pavilion (17)** surrounded by four smaller pavilions. The bust of a famous figure in Taiwan's history occupies each pavilion: Lien Ya-tang, historian of Taiwan; Chiu Feng-chia, who fought against the Japanese in the Sino-Japanese War of 1895; Liu Ming-chuan, Taiwan's first governor, and Koxinga, the famous Ming Dynasty general who chased the Dutch off the island. North of the pavilions along the path that runs near the street is another **memorial arch (18)**, erected in 1882.

The domed building at the main gate is the **Taiwan Provincial Museum (19)**, a neo-Greek structure with fluted Doric columns built in 1915 by the Japanese. There is an art gallery on the first floor and a small anthropological museum on the second floor. The entrance fee is NT$5. In the lobby of the museum are huge columns on marble bases which form the foundations for the building's huge stained-glass dome.

When you leave the museum, turn left through the **small gate (20)** that leads to the other side of the park. Here you can usually find artists at work and people practicing martial arts or dancing. In the far northwest corner are two locomotives, the first ones used in China. One was built in England in 1872 and the other in Germany in 1887. Both were retired in the 1920s. Next to the trains are several old cannons and machine guns.

Leave the park through the main gate on Hsiang Yang Road, turn left and proceed to the intersection of **Chung Ching South Road (21)**. There are a large number of book stores on this street. Continue straight to Chung Hsiao East Road and turn left again to the **North Gate (22)**. Built in 1882, the North Gate is the only one of the four remaining gates that has retained its original appearance from the Ching Dynasty. Unfortunately, an overpass was built here, crisscrossing the gate and spoiling the view of the gate.

Cross the street to Chung Hwa Road which runs along the train tracks. The road leads into the famous **Chung Hwa Market (23)**, also known as Hagler's Alley or the China Bazaar. A wide variety of small shops selling antiques, coins and stamps, clothes, electronics items and computers, tapes and records, and food, as well as numerous fortune-tellers, tailors and more line this eight-block long row of three-story structures.

The buildings are all connected, so you can walk through them without crossing any streets. If you are hungry at this point, try the Genuine Peking

Restaurant, located in the seventh row on the second floor. As its name implies, it's noted for its Peking duck. There are also a number of small restaurants serving dumplings and other snacks.

On the second floor of block eight is a store which sells costumes and items for Peking Opera, and is said to be the only place left on the island that still makes shoes for the opera performances.

Although the China Bazaar looks dingy now, it was one of the most popular shopping centers in the city in bygone days. In the past, people from all around the island who disembarked from trains at the nearby central station would make a beeline straight for the bazaar.

Refugees from mainland China, who flooded Taiwan after the communist takeover, first settled the area. Temporary houses were hastily fabricated along the railroad tracks to accommodate these people and before long more than 1,600 shacks filled with people littered the site between North Gate and South Gate.

When the number of residents grew peddlers began to congregate here and the situation started getting worse. Therefore the late President Chiang Kai-shek ordered the area to be redeveloped to provide proper housing for its inhabitants. The present block of buildings was completed in 1961.

The **traffic circle (24)** anchors the capital's well-known Hsimen District. Crowded with fast-food shops, restaurants, movie theaters and clothing stores, Hsimen, which means West Gate, was the site of the former gate that was torn down during the Japanese Occupation. From Hsimen, you can proceed to the **South Gate (25)** and on to the **Little South Gate (26)**, the last of the five city gates that were once joined together by the old city wall during the Ching Dynasty.

TIHUA STREET. Although the "good old days" are long gone, Tihua Street, one of Taipei's oldest districts, retains some of the atmosphere of yesteryear. Several shops still turn out handmade goods, so a walk through the area provides an opportunity for a glimpse of what life was like in old Taipei.

In the late 19th century, the area was the largest trading center in Taiwan and many stores are more than 100 years old. The street is extremely narrow, reputedly because it was designed for rickshaws. On holidays — especially the Chinese Lunar New Year — it's packed with shoppers.

Tihua Street is also noted for its *kulanyu* architecture, a combination of southern Chinese and European colonial styles. The red brick buildings have a store in front and a living area in the back. If you peek in one of the doorways, you will see that these buildings, though very narrow, are surprisingly long. Some even have courtyards and small gardens. Instead of standard doors, many of the houses have wooden slats that slide into place. The arched brick walkways make it possible to walk through here on one of Taipei's frequent rainy days without getting too wet. But plan your stroll for any day except Sunday, when the stores are closed.

Begin at the intersection of **Nanking West Road** and **Tihua Street (1)**. Since this tour only covers Tihua Street, it is a straight walk and virtually impossible to lose your way. Just a few blocks west are the banks of the Tamsui River where ships once unloaded their goods.

Stores on the first three blocks mainly sell cloth, although there are a few specializing in Buddhist religious items for use in temples, during festivals, and on family altars.

Three blocks north of Nanking West Road, you will see a large white-tiled building on the right. This is the new **Yung Le Market (2)**, a modern city market where urban Chinese housewives do their shopping. A wide variety of fruit, vegetables and meat are sold on the first floor, and, if you like your poultry guaranteed fresh, live chickens are kept in cages for butchering on the spot. On the second floor, there are more than 100 stands selling different kinds of textiles. You can buy material here for suits, dresses (including the sexy, slit-to-the-thigh Chinese *chipaos*), cotton-padded blankets, curtains and other uses.

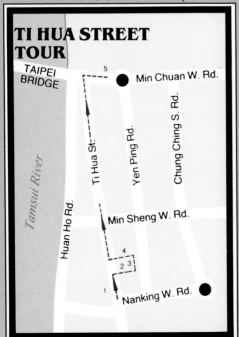

TI HUA STREET TOUR

TAIPEI BRIDGE

Tamsui River

Min Chuan W. Rd.

Ti Hua St.

Yen Ping Rd.

Chung Ching S. Rd.

Huan Ho Rd.

Min Sheng W. Rd.

Nanking W. Rd.

When you come back to the first floor walk out the rear entrance where an **old market (3)** still operates, directly opposite the modern market. You will find several stores there that process and sell fresh Chinese herbs.

Back on Tihua Street, the next building on your right is the small and unimposing **Cheng Huang Miao (4)**, or Temple of the City God, built in 1859. Worship of the City God dates back even further, to the legendary Emperor Yao, who is reputed to have reigned from B C 2357 to 2255. Needless to say the City God is in charge of Taipei, basically working in heaven in the same capacity as the local magistrate, or *Yamen*, would in the world of mortals. That's why the temple layout resembles that of a city magistrate. The birthday celebration of the City God, on the 13th day of the fifth lunar month (usually in June), is one of the biggest festivals held annually in Taipei.

In front of the temple hang several hundred lanterns. People praying for peace donated them. Inside on the main altar, you will see about 200 statues of gods. That's more than most any other temple on the island. The statues also have been donated to the temple by Buddhist worshipers to thank the gods for answering their prayers.

The two mean-looking deities to the right and left of the altar are General Hsieh and General Fan, the City God's bodyguards. According to local lore, the two men were close friends who lived in Fukien Province. One day, they were caught in a heavy rainstorm. Hsieh, the tall one, volunteered to get an umbrella to shield the two from the rain. However, when a flood rose, Fan, who was waiting beside a stream, drowned. When Hsieh returned and found his friend dead he was so sad he hung himself. Since General Fan drowned he is painted black, while General Hsieh is in white garments with his tongue hanging out a foot long, a sardonic reminder of his method of suicide. When the statues of these dieties are carried in processions, Hsieh is seen carrying a large, folded umbrella over his shoulder.

Turn right when you exit the temple and continue north on Tihua Street. Stores on both sides of the next several blocks sell spices, Chinese medicine, and dried herbs from mainland China and other countries. Here, you'll see Chinese druggists chopping and grinding various herbs and medicines and wrapping them in newspaper cones for customers to take home.

Because this walk takes you only as far as the Taipei Bridge, all of the following shop numbers refer to Section 1. Look for even numbers on the right, odd on the left.

There is a coffin maker's shop with huge slabs of lumber out front at **No. 174**. The Chinese make coffins out of tree trunks, rounded at the top. They

are often carved and painted in rich colors. According to a sign over the door of the Lin Feng Yi Shop at **No. 214**, the family began selling bamboo and wooden utensils in 1906. The store sells a variety of baskets, buckets and bamboo steamers.

An array of hand-painted paper and plastic lanterns in many shapes and sizes can be found at **No. 310**, one of the few places in the capital that manufactures the lanterns it sells. Although the lanterns are made in a factory elsewhere in the city, the painting is done on the premises. The shop has been in business in the same location for more than 80 years, and is now run by the third generation family members.

The shop at **Nos. 303-305** sells Chinese cooking utensils. It's crammed with woks, bowls, plates, steamers, clay pots and other kitchen items. Just a few doors away at **No. 333** is a man who makes cotton-padded blankets by hand right out front. Blankets can be made-to-order. The price depends on the weight of the cotton used.

There is an old-fashioned ice factory at **No. 345**, reminiscent of days when big blocks of ice were delivered door-to-door for use in ice boxes. Huge blocks are slid out of the small factory and onto trucks standing just outside.

When you reach the Taipei Bridge on **Minchwan West Road (5)**, turn right. Here you will see several local artisans at work carving wooden Buddhist statues and hand-sculpted stone carvings. This marks the end of the tour, but if you're not too tired, you may want to walk back down Tihua Street to explore the nooks and crannies some of the small streets that cut through it.

SEVEN STAR MOUNTAIN. Yangmingshan National Park, which became Taiwan's third national park in 1985, covers a total area of 11,000 hectares. The park has 20 dormant volcanos that are from 400,000 to 1.2 million years old, countless hot springs and geysers, 1,200 varieties of plants, many of which are found only in Taiwan or at high altitudes, 130 species of butterflies, 59 different kinds of birds, 12 types of frogs and five species of squirrels to name a few.

This walking tour will take you to one of the park's premier attractions, Seven Star Mountain, among other unique features. Be sure to bring rain gear, because frequent downpours drench the mountain. You should also bring some food and water along, because there are no eating facilities along this route.

The walk begins at **Sungyuan**. To get there, you can take a taxi straight from downtown Taipei for about NT$250. If you choose the bus, take the No. 301 or the No. 260 which depart one block east of the Hilton Hotel on Chung Hsiao West Road. The ride takes about 40 minutes. Get off at **Chinese**

Culture University and change here to a taxi for the four kilometer ride to Sungyuan. If you have time, take the road directly opposite the Seven-Eleven Store, which takes about an hour.

The ride up the winding ridge roads of Yangmingshan is the first attraction. It provides an excellent view overlooking the city and a fleeting glimpse of several classes of houses. Yangmingshan is home to wealthy Chinese and to expatriates working for foreign companies, as well as to ordinary Chinese families who have lived there for generations. Along the way, you will pass modern villas and traditional Chinese country houses.

The first destination on the walking tour is **Menghuanhu**, the Dream Lake. It's situated on a lower level of Seven Star Mountain. During this 15-minute stretch, you'll pass a fork in the road; keep left and continue walking until you see a small road sign on the left side of the road. Follow the stone steps up the hill behind the sign that says Dream Lake.

A few minutes later you will arrive at a small pavilion, left of the path. Benches make it a good place for a breather or lunch.

When you return to the stone path, continue back up the mountain. You will soon come to a level area where another road stretches to your left. A sign here indicates that Dream Lake is 100 meters ahead

and that a path leading up Seven Star Mountain is 900 meters away. Walk on to the lake for now, but don't forget the route because you will retrace your steps later for the walk up the mountain.

A second pavilion a few minutes walk from the crossroads is a two-story structure that on a clear day affords a panoramic view of the Taipei basin and the winding Keelung and Tamsui Rivers. Take the path behind the pavilion for the final trek to Dream Lake. The lake, 864 meters above sea level, is noted for 50 species of plant including a rare water scallion that is protected from pickers in a conservation area.

Dream Lake covers an area of 800 square meters and is just two meters deep. It is actually a volcanic crater filled with rain water. In the summer, two-thirds of the lake is covered with vegetation. In the winter, it serves as home to waterfowl that migrate from mainland China.

Formerly called Duck Pond, the lake later became known as *menghua*, literally dream or illusion in English, because fog and mist often enshrouds the area, giving the lake and nearby areas a magically moody atmosphere.

After taking in Dream Lake, retrace your steps back to the fork in the road that leads further up Seven Star Mountain. It takes its name from seven small peaks on the summit of this classically-shaped conical volcano. The mountain last erupted 300,000 years ago in the most recent of three series of eruptions on the Tatun Mountain Range. Seven Star Mountain, 1,120 meters above sea level, is the highest peak in the range and the highest point in the Taipei area. It's also one of the few places in Taiwan that gets snowed on in winter.

While the path up the mountain is not difficult to walk, it narrows at some points. Because it's not paved, be prepared to occasionally walk over rocks and high grass. If you find the path up the mountain too difficult, return to Dream Lake and head down the path to the Yangmingshan-Jinshan Highway. When you reach the bottom of the hill turn left down the road past the military base and look for a roadside pavilion. Around the corner from it you can catch a highway bus back to Taipei. Don't walk back to Sungyuan unless you want to walk all the way back to Shantzuhuou. There are no buses passing through Sungyuan.

If you do continue up the mountain, about halfway up you will encounter **sulfur steam geysers** ranging in temperature from 90 to 120 degrees centigrade. The water is hot enough to boil an egg within five minutes, which is what many visitors do. The largest of the geysers spouts up to 100 meters. As a result of the mineral deposits left by the geysers and streams, the side of the mountain is covered with spots of red, yellow, black and white.

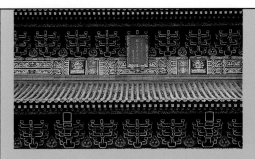

Once you reach the top of Seven Star Mountain take the path that leads down to **Miaopu**. From here you can catch a bus back to Taipei. If you have trouble finding the path to Miaopu, just take any route down the mountain. You will find buses heading for the city wherever you end up on the main highway.

WANHUA. This tour takes you to some of this famous areas most famous temples, and up and down alleys and side streets that provide a glimpse of one of the capital's few surviving traditional Taiwanese neighborhoods. It begins at the intersection of **Kwang Chow Street** and **Hwanho South Road (1)**, not far from the banks of the Tamsui River where boats sailing from mainland China unloaded goods during the Ching Dynasty.

One block south of Kwang Chow Street is the **Hsuehai Academy of Classical Learning (2)** founded in 1837, the only establishment of its kind still intact in the city. When the structure was an academy, the main hall was a lecture room, the rear hall was dedicated to Chu Hsi (1130-1200), the Chinese philosopher of neo-Confucianism, and the side wings served as a dormitory for teachers and students of the academy.

During the colonial period the Japanese confiscated the building and turned it into an army barracks. Later it became a Japanese langauge school. A man named Gao, who was impressed with the temple's good fengshui and the fact that it formerly served as a school for classical studies eventually bought the property and converted it into the Gao Ancestral Temple. When Hwanho South Road was broadened, the temple was renovated and so unfortunately no longer looks like the original structure.

Double back to the entrance to Kwang Chow Street and walk down the first alley on the left to the **Hwang family shrine (3)**, which dates to the 1830s. This temple was also recently renovated and covered with fresh paint, making it look much younger than it really is. The huge beams and other wooden parts under all that paint were shipped from mainland China more than 150 years ago.

On the main altar are dozens of ancestral tablets placed there by families who share the surname Hwang. There are also numerous colorful murals on the walls that depict famous stories from Chinese history. The temple houses a nursery school and small children can be seen laughing and playing in the courtyard.

When you leave the temple turn right, walk one block down to Hwanho South Road and turn right at the first lane. One block in and on the right you

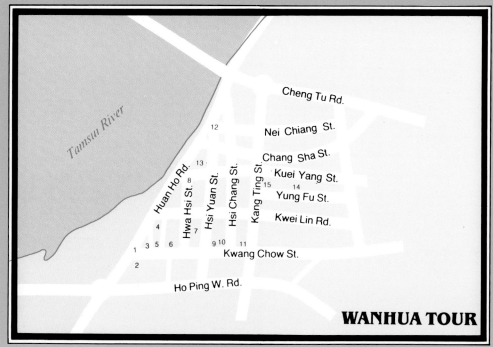

WANHUA TOUR

will see the **Chitian Temple (4)** of 1786. It is said to be the only temple in the Wanhua area dedicated to Matsu, Goddess of the Sea and patron saint of Chinese sailors.

According to a popular story, in the late 1700s when Mongka engaged in extensive commerce with mainland China, there was a vessel known as the Red Ship which transported timber. Once, while at sea, the Red Ship suddenly ran into a storm. The ship's frightened crew prayed to Matsu to protect them. Miraculously, it escaped harm, and safely reached shore. To thank the goddess for her holy intervention, people built a temple to worship her in what was then a timber yard.

Originally made of wood, the temple has been rebuilt several times and is now mainly concrete. Matsu sits on the main altar wearing a crown made of strings of pearls. To the right and left are her fierce bodyguards. The green one is General Thousand Miles and the red one is General Favorable Winds.

Turn left when you exit the temple and continue down the lane until you come out again on Kwang Chow Street. Families still occupy the old traditional-style red brick Chinese houses here.

When you get to Kwang Chow Street turn left again. In the evening, this busy market area has a carnival atmosphere. Hundreds of peddlers sell food and goods galore. On the left side of the street is a restaurant that specializes in venison. Animal lovers beware: sometimes you'll see live deers caged nearby while another is being butchered on the spot. Snake dishes are also prepared here in the evening at little roadside stands.

One block ahead on the right is the old **Renji Hospital (5)**, the site of the former Mongka Foundling Hospital. In 1870, donations were solicited from wealthy businessmen in the Mongka area for the construction of a hospital for abandoned children and the children of people too poor to raise them. During the Occupation, the Japanese forced the people to turn it into Renji Hospital. They destroyed the former building. Of the original foundling hospital, only the granite tablet at the front door remains.

Next on the left is the infamous **Hwa Hsi Street**, better known as **Snake Alley (6)**. Unfortunately, in an attempt to beautify the area, the city government turned the street into the Hwa Hsi Tourist Night Market in 1987. The street was covered and many of its store fronts modernized, diluting Snake Alley's formerly pungent flavor. However, many of its restaurants continue to serve snake, turtle and other gourmet dishes. The method of preparation is cruel and not a recommended sightseeing attraction for those with weak stomachs.

Toward the end of Section A on the right, you'll find the street's most famous restaurant, **Tainan Tan Tsu Mien (7)**. With its baroque glass chandeliers, French provincial carpets, white columns and gold-trimmed ceilings, this expensive seafood palace seems out of place amid the somewhat rundown surroundings. Food is served on expensive English china and water poured into crystal glasses. The padded stools around each table are the only concession to local tastes.

A bit beyond Section B is Taipei's most notorious **Red Light District (8)**. On the left-hand side, a maze of winding side streets are the haunt of an estimated 1,000 prostitutes who loiter in front of red-lit doorways attempting to lure men into the tiny rooms of their brothels.

Walk back down Hwa Hsi Street to Kwang Chow Street and turn left. After you cross the first major intersection, you'll see the **Lungshan Temple (9)**. Beyond the second gate, people throw divining blocks to determine their fortune and make fruit offerings to the gods. Further inside, at the main and rear altars, people burn incense at large brass urns.

The Goddess of Mercy sits on the main altar surrounded by other gods. To the rear, there's another altar set up to house Taoist deities like Matsu, the Goddess of the Sea. On the roof of the main hall is a pagoda that represents the staircase to heaven. The temple is also renowned for its stone sculptures, especially the 12 columns with the dragons wound around them, wood carvings, and bronze work.

Turn left after leaving the temple and take another left at the first lane. At this **herb market (10)**, pungent medicinal roots and plants are on sale. Walk straight through across Hsi Chang Street and enter the front yard of the **Ti Tsang Wang Temple (11)** where you can join others in worshiping the rulers of hell. In the evening, a clothes night market sets up on this section of the street.

Walk down Hsi Chang Street to Neichiang Street and turn left. A few blocks away is a small park with a temple on one side. This is the **Fu Te Temple (12)**, which was established in the 1930s for the worship of the Earth God . The temple was originally on Hsi Chang Street and shifted to its new location recently. It originally was part of a gate which was locked at night to protect residents from attack by bandits, pirates and rebel forces. Hundreds of statues of the Earth God have been left here temporarily by local people who are away from home and cannot worship him properly.

Follow Hsi Yuan Street to Kuei Yang Street. One block to the right is the **Ching Shan Temple (13)**, founded in 1856, and known for its fine carvings. This temple is dedicated to General Chang of the Three Kingdoms Period (A.D. 220-265). He was later deified.

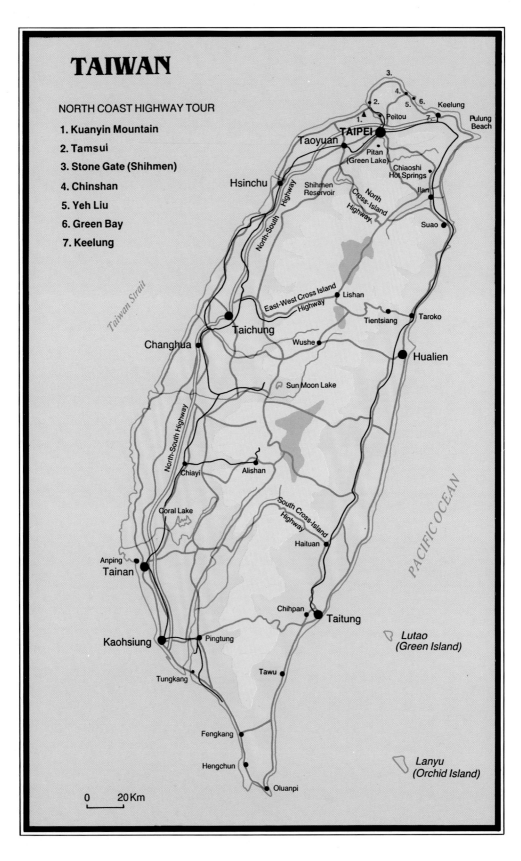

TAIWAN

NORTH COAST HIGHWAY TOUR

1. **Kuanyin Mountain**
2. **Tamsui**
3. **Stone Gate (Shihmen)**
4. **Chinshan**
5. **Yeh Liu**
6. **Green Bay**
7. **Keelung**

Keelung

Pulung Beach

Peitou

TAIPEI

Taoyuan

Pitan (Green Lake)

Chiaoshi Hot Springs

Hsinchu

Shihmen Reservoir

North Cross-Island Highway

Ilan

Suao

Taiwan Strait

East-West Cross Island Highway

Lishan

Tientsiang

Taroko

Taichung

Wushe

Changhua

Hualien

Sun Moon Lake

North-South Highway

Chiayi

Alishan

Coral Lake

South Cross-Island Highway

Haituan

PACIFIC OCEAN

Anping

Tainan

Chihpan

Taitung

Kaohsiung

Pingtung

Lutao (Green Island)

Tawu

Tungkang

Fengkang

Lanyu (Orchid Island)

Hengchun

Oluanpi

0   20 Km

According to legend, a statue of this god was being transported from Fukien to a temple in Taiwan in 1854. After reaching shore in Taiwan, the people carrying the statue to its new home suddenly found they were unable to move it any further when they reached a spot on Hsi Yuan Street. Divining blocks used to determine the cause of this phenomenon indicated that the god wanted to have the temple built on the site.

Shortly after that an epidemic broke out in the area and it is said that everyone who prayed at the new temple was saved. This story made the temple famous. More and more believers came here to worship. Two years later the temple was moved to its present site to accommodate the crush.

Next walk down Kuei Yang St, passing under the round red-brick archways and past the numerous fruit and food stalls. At Section 2, No. 94, you'll find the gleaming and modern **Mongka Church (14)**, looking a bit overdressed among its much older neighbors.

This is the site of an old Mongka Church built in 1879 by George Leslie Mackay, a Canadian missionary. Until the latter part of the Ching Dynasty, people in Mongka were very anti-Christian and Mackay met strong opposition when he first arrived to preach. But he persisted and eventually succeeded in building his church, which was torn down in the mid-1980s to make way for this new structure.

Walk back to the intersection of Kangting Road and Kuei Yang, turn right and walk one block to the Temple of the Patron Saint of **Ching-Shui-Yen (15)**, built in 1790, a blend of Buddhist and Taoist elements. It is dedicated to a soldier from Hunan Province who distinguished himself in battle in southern China. After the soldier died, he was deified and worshipers built him a temple in Fukien. Tradition holds that this god was introduced to Taiwan by the soldiers of Koxinga, the famous loyalist of the Ming Dynasty (1368-1644) who attempted to use Taiwan as a base for retaking the mainland from the Manchus. The main statue of this god was brought here from the original temple on the mainland.

One of the minor gods of this temple is called the patron saint of Penglai. People from the temple say that when some event — either good or bad — is about to occur, Penglai's nose falls off as a warning sign. When the event passes, the nose automatically reattaches itself. Any attempt to put the statue's nose back on before the right time is fruitless, according to local lore. In the main temple hall, there is a large tablet that's said to have been dedicated by Emperor Kuang Hsu of the Ching Dynasty. From the temple gate you should be able to catch a taxi. Or you can turn left on Kangting Road and walk back to Kwang Chow Street, just a few blocks east of the Lungshan Temple, for another look at the temple or for a longer stroll through one of the two night markets in the area.

NORTH COAST HIGHWAY LOOP. This driving tour will take you along the Northeast Coast Highway, one of the most beautiful areas in Taiwan. It begins in the city of Tamsui, northwest of Taipei, hugs the northernmost tip of the island, then winds up in the port city of Keelung on the northeast coast. Some tour operators offer guided coach tours along the same route, but in order to enjoy the sights at your own pace, you will need to beg, borrow or rent a car.

To get to the Northeast Coast Highway, which is also known as Route 2, drive north on Chung Shan North Road to Shih Lin. After crossing the Fuilin Bridge turn left and proceed straight to Wen Lin Road which will take you to Peitou. After passing the huge Da Tung plant continue along Bai Ling Road to Kuantu where the road runs alongside the Tamsui River when you pass the Kuantu Bridge. (Make sure you don't cross the bridge.) From this point just follow the signs to Tamsui.

As you drive up the east bank of the Tamsui River towards the town, you will see **Kuanyin Mountain (1)** looming in the distance; it slopes up from the west bank and rapidly rises more than 540 meters (1,800 feet). The mountain is named after the Goddess of Mercy (which is what *Kuanyin* means in Mandarin, the predominant Chinese language in Taiwan, as well as mainland China) because the top of the mountain resembles the head of the goddess. The Tamsui River widens here where it meets the sea. This was the site of numerous naval battles when colonial powers were seeking to conquer the island.

In **Tamsui (2)** visit **Fort Santo Domingo**, which the government has designated a "historical site of the first rank." The fort is located on a ridge overlooking the Tamsui River and was built by the Spanish in 1629, as they expanded their territory from Keelung which had been occupied three years earlier.

In 1642, Tamsui fell to the Dutch and the fort became known among local Chinese as Hung Mao Cheng, the Fort of the Red-haired Barbarians. The Dutch in turn were evicted in 1662 by Koxinga, the Ming Dynasty patriot. A number of Ching Dynasty antique cannons dating from the early 19th century still stand as if ready for action under the terrace.

In 1867, the British obtained a permanent lease for the property from the Ching rulers and added a consulate there in 1891. The British remained at the fort until 1972, turning it over to the care of Australia. Within a few months Australia broke off diplomatic relations and the site was entrusted to the United States until the Taiwan government formally resumed possession in 1980.

There is an interesting 20-minute walk to the fort from the train station; it passes through a quaint fishing village where Hollywood crews filmed waterfront scenes for *The Sand Pebbles*, the epic movie that starred Steve McQueen. There are also several good seafood restaurants.

If you have time, walk up the hill on the coast to the pleasant campus of Tamkang University which overlooks the beach. The buildings on campus blend Chinese and modern architectural styles and many of the classrooms have Chinese-style eaves and peaked roofs.

From Tamsui return to Route 2 heading northeast; you will reach the ocean in about 15 minutes. The road follows the coast all the way to Keelung and you can stop to swim or fish almost anywhere along this stretch.

The next major landmark on the route is Stone Gate, or **Shihmen (3)**, which is located at the northernmost tip of the island. The area is named after a huge gap in a rock, formed over the millenia by the action of pounding waves. It marks the boundary between the Taiwan Strait to the west and the East China Sea and Pacific Ocean to the east.

From Shihmen continue along Route 2 about another 20 minutes to **Chinshan (4)**, a fishing village with a beautiful park and beach. In addition to swimming there are also facilities here for boating, water skiing, surfing and camping.

The next point of interest on the highway is **Yeh Liu (5)**, one of Taiwan's most famous sightseeing attractions, noted for its gallery of unusual rock formations. Like the Shihmen, the wind and sea carved the odd shapes into the rocks through the ages. The formations are particularly popular with amateur and professional photographers and have been given names based on their shapes including the Queen's Head, which looks a bit like an Egyptian monarch, Cinderella's Slipper, and Dinosaur.

Yeh Liu takes its name from the adjoining fishing village where you can visit Ocean World, an aquatic park with trained dolphins, other sea mammals and diving acts.

Next, the tour route passes through **Green Bay (6)**, a city about two miles east of Yeh Liu. It has an excellent beach and equipment rentals for windsurfing, para-sailng, hang gliding, sailing, scuba diving, and fishing. In addition, there is an amusement park for children and several dozen bungalows that can be rented along the beach.

The last stop on the tour is the busy port city of **Keelung (7)** which overlooks the East China Sea. Keelung, the second largest port in Taiwan boasts some interesting scenery, but its history is even more fascinating.

The Spanish first landed in the area in 1626 when they were searching for a natural harbor from which to expand their trade in the Far East. The Spanish named the city Santissima Trinidad and built a large number of forts, which have since been destroyed. At that time, only a small number of Chinese and aborigines lived in Keelung, which was then a hiding place for Japanese pirates. The Spanish were defeated 18 months later by the Dutch who ruled the city until 1662 when it was finally returned to China. Keelung remained in Chinese hands until 1884 when the French occupied it for eight months. The city was lost yet again in 1895 when Japan defeated China in the Sino-Japanese War.

From green Chungcheng Park, you can get a panoramic view of the harbor clogged with rusty freighters and the gray boxy buildings of the city. Finding the park is no problem; there's a conspicious white, 22-meter (74-foot) statue of the Goddess of Mercy perched on the top of the mountain that can be seen from almost anywhere in Keelung.

For an even better view, however, especially at night, climb up the steps inside the statue. Many old cannons, as well as buildings from the Ching Dynasty and Japanese occupation, still can be found in the park overlooking the harbor. At the foot of the hill is a cemetery where French soldiers killed during the attack on Keelung are buried. The French government still maintains the cemetery.

On the mountain opposite the Grave of the National Heroes at Ta-sha-wan is the Erh-sha-wan Gun Emplacement. At the beginning of the Opium War in 1840 the British were planning to attack Taiwan and the local magistrate ordered the construction of the parapet to improve the island's defenses. They installed a battery of eight cannons at the location, which provided wide coverage for their gunners and, of course, an excellent harbor view for modern-day visitors.

The British army's first attack occurred in August, 1841, but the local army, under the command of the Manchu general, Ta-hung-ah, put up strong resistance, sinking several enemy warships and taking a number of British prisoners. In 1843, after several unsuccessful attempts to seize Taiwan, the British called it quits.

From Keelung, the Japanese managed to extend their control to the whole island and ruled Taiwan until 1945 when they surrendered to the Allies in World War II.

Keelung is a busy port where ships from around the world can be seen. The city also has several good restaurants, but you might want to try its night market instead. It specializes in fresh seafood caught in the local waters.

This point marks the end of the tour. From Keelung, it's an easy 30 to 40 minute drive back to Taipei via the North-South Highway which takes you back full circle.

Off the Beaten Track

THE KWANG HWA MARKET. Under the Kwang Hwa Bridge at the intersection of Shinsheng South Road and Pateh Road. Old Chinese and foreign language books and magazines, inexpensive computers and electronic items, handicrafts and rare Chinese antiques can sometimes be found in this intriguing bazaar.

TEAHOUSES, once the reserve of old men, have made a comeback in Taiwan in recent years (see **Tea for You**). Among the best are:

Tungpo, designed in traditional style with red brick walls, cobblestone floors and room mats. The folk artifacts displayed here were found by owners who searched outlying villages for bowls, statues, stone, wood-carvings and temple accessories. Birds fly freely around as you sip your tea. Customers must use a wooden ladle to get their own hot water from a traditional stove. At 784 Ding Chow Rd.

Wisteria, located near National Taiwan University, the pioneer of the teahouse revival in Taipei. This is an old Japanese-style house with hundreds of potted plants in its back and front yards. Since the floors are covered with tatami mats, shoes must be removed upon entering. At No. 1, Alley 16, Shinsheng S Rd., Sec. 3.

Cafe Vernai, located in an office building, provides both tables and tatami rooms. The decor is a cross between Japanese and Chinese. On the 2nd Fl., 110 Jenai Rd., Sec. 4.

The Teahouse Dining Theater holds a variety of lectures and Chinese performances, including storytelling, musical programs, plays and puppet shows.

TZUSHIH TEMPLE, located in the small village of Sanhsia, about 22 kilometers from Taipei has been under reconstruction since 1947 and the work is expected to continue until 1995. This temple is noted for its wood and stone carving and is said to be one of the best examples of temple arts in Taiwan. The village was the headquarters of the anti-Japanese resistance in northern Taiwan after the Japanese Occupation began in 1895. In retaliation, the Japanese burned the temple down. During World II, the temple was destroyed again by allied bombers. The temple was originally built in 1787 and still contains Buddhist relics brought over from Fukien Province. Some of the island's best carvers work at the back of the temple and visitors are welcome to watch them as they practice their craft. Sanhsia, which has retained a great deal of Ching Dynasty architecture, is also worth the visit. The village looks much as it did at the turn of the century with rows of brick houses lining narrow streets.

BUDDHIST VEGETARIAN LUNCH at the Yuan Tung Temple, a Buddhist nunnery. The temple provides vegetarian meals every afternoon. Pay what you like. Located in Chung Ho, just 20 minutes by taxi from downtown Taipei.

HOT SPRINGS. Soak in one of the island's more than 100 hot sulfur springs. The Whispering Pines Inn, in nearby Peitou, is decorated in Japanese style, complete with traditional straw mats, sliding screen doors, and a Japanese garden. Each room has its own natural spring, in addition to the communal pool. Sunmoon Restaurant, has wooden rooms with hot spring baths for two people as well as several large outdoor pools. The baths are in the midst of a grove of trees with walkways, providing an excellent atmosphere for taking a sulfur bath. Rustic, but clean. Located halfway down from the summit of Yangmingshan on the way to Jinshan on the Jinshan-Yangmingshan Road.

FU HSING CHINESE OPERA MUSEUM, at the National Fu Hsing Dramatic Arts Academy, displays all kinds of Chinese opera equipment, including colorful costumes, headgear, weapons and musical instruments. Visitors are shown a film on opera and then receive a guided tour of the displays led by one of the performers. After touring the museum visitors may watch a performance at the school, one of two of its kind in Taiwan. The museum is only open on Tuesday and Thursday, and Saturday mornings, and at present only accepts group tours because of its personnel shortage. If you would like to visit and see one of these performances call the school at 790-0234. The school's address is 177 Neihu Rd., Sec. 2.

TAIPEI NEW PARK is the place to go to watch the Chinese at play. Activities begin at around sunrise as peddlers lay out their goods including herbs, ointments, tea, socks, shoes, pens and nail clippers on pieces of cloth on the sidewalk in front of the park. Hundreds of people, both young and old, come to the park every morning for some excercise before heading off to work or school. Among the popular ways of working out are various forms of martial arts, modern and ballroom dancing, calisthenics and badminton.

LIN AN-TAI MANSION, a classic example of traditional Ching Dynasty architecture, was originally located on Swei Road, but was rebuilt in Pinchiang Park in 1978 to make way for the expansion of Tunhua South Road. After five months of painstaking effort, the structure was taken apart piece-by-piece. It then took workers 20 months to reassemble the 20,982 planks and beams, 38,096 bricks, 240,050 tiles, 95 windows and 32 large wood carvings.

YANGMINSHAN NATIONAL PARK is just 30 minutes from downtown Taipei and has long been a favorite getaway for city residents. The park is famous for its waterfalls, sulfur springs, fountains and cherry blossoms which bloom during the spring flower season. The park is an excellent place for hiking and provides a nice view of the Taipei basin.

THE CHINA POTTERY ARTS COMPANY will let you watch their craftsmen producing pottery and porcelain at its factory in Peitou. An adjoining showroom displays hundreds of items for sale.

KUANTU NATURAL PARK, situated at the point where the Tamsui River and Keelung River meet, is an ideal place to watch the many migratory birds that winter in Taiwan. The park is divided into several sections including an ecological preserve, recreation area and bird sanctuary.

THE TAIWAN FOLK ART MUSEUM is a Tang Dynasty style building that has a selection of Chinese and aborigine crafts on display and for sale. There are also an adjoining teahouse, Mongolian Bar-B-Q Restaurant and hot spring facilities. At 32 You Ya Rd., Peitou, 894-7185.

VISIT THE HOLIDAY FLOWER MARKET under the Chienkuo North-South elevated highway, between Hsin Yi Road and Jen Ai Road. Hundreds of vendors selling a wide variety of plants and supplies. Open Saturdays and Sundays from 8 a.m. to 5 p.m.

THE LIN FAMILY GARDEN was built on the eve of the Sino-Japanese War in 1894 and considered by literati to be "the most picturesque garden in northern Taiwan." The 12,000-square meter garden was built by a wealthy rice merchant who immigrated to Taiwan from Fukien Province. When the Japanese occupied the island, the Lins fled to the mainland and the garden was used by Japanese officials as a villa. The garden was seriously damaged by refugees who squatted there after World War II. Restoration work, begun in 1982, was completed in 1986 at a cost of U.S.$4.5 million. It is located in the surburb of Panchiao and is open Tuesday through Sunday from 9 a.m. to 5 p.m. Admission is NT$60.

JADE can be purchased at the Kwang Hwa Jade Market, at the intersection of Pateh Road and Hsinsheng South Road, where hundreds of dealers set up tables every Sunday. Quality varies greatly, so be careful when buying.

NIGHT MARKETS. A wide variety of inexpensive items and local snacks can be found at night markets around Taipei and, with their carnival atmosphere, can make for an interesting adventure. There are no fixed prices here, so be prepared to bargain. The Shihlin Night Market, Taipei's biggest, is just a few kilometers north of the Grand Hotel; Snake Alley Night Market, near the Lungshan Temple, and the Jao-ho Tourist Night Market. The Jao-ho Night Market is Taipei's newest. The 500-meter long market is divided into three sections. The eastern section near the Tzuyu Temple has about 100 stands selling clothing, fruit and toys. In the western section there are about 40 food vendors and in the central section there are a number of Chinese folk artists and performers.

TEMPLE OF THE GOLDEN BUDDHA. In 1954 Abbot Tzu Hang, a well-known Buddhist monk, died at the age of 60. Following his instructions, his upright body was placed in an urn which was buried for four years. When the urn was unearthed and opened it was discovered that his body was preserved mummy-like, despite the fact that no embalming methods were used. The body was covered with gold leaf and now sits in the Temple of the Golden Buddha, in Hsichi, a Taipei suburb.

FOR A NIGHT OUT explore the area around the National Taiwan University campus. There is a small night market along Roosevelt Road, opposite the university, and numerous restaurants, bookstores and gift shops in the surrounding streets. Have dinner at one of the Southeast Asian restaurants (Indonesia, Thai, Burmese, and Vietnamese) all closely located on Dingchow Road, which runs parallel to Roosevelt, then relax in the Tungpo Teahouse, 784 Ding Chow Rd., or the Blues Cafe, 2nd Fl., No. 2, Lane 52, Roosevelt Rd, a coffee shop with a collection of jazz recordings.

VISIT AN ABORIGINAL VILLAGE in Wulai, the home of some 3,000 aborigines of the Atayal Tribe. Wulai is a resort area about one hour from Taipei. Aborigines here put on dance shows, but the performances are a bit commercial. To see a genuine village take the bus from the main Wulai Station to Hsinhsien Village. Bring your passport and apply for a pass from the police station next to the bus station. Buses leave Wulai at 6:30 a.m., 12:30 p.m. and 5 p.m.

PICK FRUIT at one of Taipei's five suburban tourist farms. A small fee is charged to enter the orange and strawberry farms. There is no charge for tasting, but a price is charged for fruit taken out of the farm.

The Peitou Orange Farm, 18 kilometers from Taipei, welcomes visitors to wander through the groves with knife and plastic bag in hand to pick oranges and strawberries. Take Bus No. 218 to Peitou and transfer to the smaller No. 7 or No. 9 bus for Chywan Yuan Li. Open from January to April.

The Mucha Tea Garden, is famous for its Iron Goddess tea. The garden does not permit visitors to pick tea themselves because of the difficulty in selecting leaves and because the leaves must go through several stages of drying and processing before it is ready for consumption. However, paths through the fields are open to visitors who are free to watch the farmers at work harvesting and planting the crop. You can also sample the different kinds of local tea and buy it here cheaper than in the city. Take Bus No. 251 or 236 to the last stop, National Chengchi University, and change to the smaller No. 10 bus which goes right to the farm. Open from 10 a.m. to 4:30 p.m.

Best Bets

BREAKFAST at the Chinese Tea House in the basement of the Grand Hotel. This small restaurant, furnished with simple but elegant square wooden tables and stools, offers tea and excellent, but inexpensive, Chinese snacks such as steamed dumplings, *paotzu*, wonton, noodles and pastries. After eating take a leisurely walk around the hotel and the grounds behind the hotel.

ACUPUNCTURE. Information on acupuncture treatment and training can be obtained at the China Acupuncture Association, 4th Floor, 66-1, Chungking S Rd., Sec. 1, Tel. 331-2468.

BOOKSHOPS with the best selection of low-priced English books are Caves, 103 Chungshan N Rd., Sec. 2, 537-1666; Lin Kou Book, Sound and Gift Co., 54-3 Chungshan N Rd., Sec. 3, 595-1565; and, the Lucky Bookstore, 129-1 Hoping E Rd, Sec. 1 (inside Taiwan Normal University), 391-3552.

PAPAYA MILKSHAKES that taste better than ice cream milkshakes can be sampled at fruit stands throughout the city.

FOR AN INTERESTING DISCUSSION of controversial topics in the news, listen to Issues and Opinions, Monday nights at 8:30 on International Community Radio Taiwan, FM 100.

ANTIQUES can be purchased under the Kwang Hwa Market Bridge at the intersection of Shinsheng South Road and Pateh Road and the Chung Hwa Market on Chung Hwa Road. Bear in mind, however, that there are few antique bargains in Taiwan and more than a few phoney pieces floating around, so excercise caution before buying.

ICE CREAM SUNDAES are built the American way at Swensen's, 109 Jen Ai Rd., Sec. 4, 218 Tunhua N Rd.

TSIENTIN RUGS. Taiwan is one of the few remaining places in the world where Tientsin rugs are still being handmade. These hand-knotted carpets are named after the North China port of Tientsin, once the leading producer of Chinese carpets. Many of the designs are patterned after carpets woven for the floor of the Imperial Palace in Peking. The rugs, which are composed of 100 percent wool, take months of complex hand-knotting to complete. Visit the government-run Veteran Rug and Blanket Manufacturing Co., 2-4 Lane 27, Chungshan N Rd., Sec. 2, Tel. 541-2519. Shipping can be arranged. Carpets ordered for export are cheaper because the wool import duty need not be paid.

HELPFUL BOOK for people moving to Taipei is *Quest for the Best* in Taiwan by Dorothy Orr Cole. It incorporates all you need to know about living on the island.

THE CULTURAL PALACE bills itself as the largest barber shop in the world. It has about 200 barber chairs, private and semi-private rooms named after places in mainland China, and provides a wide range of services for both men and women, including face and body massage, and finger and toe manicures, as well as standard haircuts.

CUSTOM-MADE SUITS AND SHIRTS are inexpensive in Taiwan and some of the best tailors have outlets in the major hotels. There are also a number of tailors in the area along Linsen North Road near the President and Ambassador Hotels. A two-piece custom-made suit sells for about NT$6,000 and shirts for NT$600.

CHINESE OPERA performances are held at the Sun Yat-sen Memorial Hall, Jen Ai Rd., Sec. 4, every Saturday afternoon at 2 p.m. and 4 p.m. Admission is free. Opera can also be seen at the Armed Forces Cultural Activities Center, 69 Chung Hwa Rd., opposite Section 7 of the China Market. Performances are usually at 7:30 p.m. and tickets sell for NT$100-300.

HANDICRAFTS can be found at the Taiwan Crafts Center, 7th Floor, 110 Yenping N. Rd. and the Taiwan Handicraft Promotion Center, 1 Hsu Chow Rd. These two stores offer an array of popular products such as ceramic ware, pottery with traditional-style designs, jewelry including the ever popular jade, bamboo, rattan, marble and wood items, brassware and cloisonne.

CALLIGRAPHY TOOLS, also known as the "Four Treasures of the Studio," include the writing brush, inkstone, inkstick and paper. A wide variety of writing tools, many of which are artistic in themselves, can be found in shops along Chungching South Road. Kander Co., 25 Chunghsiao W Rd., Sec. 1, just a few blocks east of the Hilton Hotel, has a large selection of these items.

THE CHIPAO, better known by the Cantonese word *cheongsam*, with its mandarin collar, hip-hugging fit and deep side-slit, is the traditional Chinese evening gown. Many contemporary versions of the *chipao* are now available and may be worn for any occasion. Numerous sewing shops can be found on Poai Road, Hengyang Road and in the Hsimen district. Most have special departments for tailoring *chipaos* made of silk, satin and other materials. Slip into a *chipao* and fancy yourself as Suzie Wong.

WHERE TO FIND OUT WHAT'S GOING ON AROUND TOWN. *Bang* magazine, an arts and leisure monthly for expatriates, lists upcoming events. Also check the community pages in the two English dailies, *The China Post* and *China News*.

CHINESE FOOD. An almost unimaginable variety of cuisines originated in China. And Taipei has an almost unimaginable number of restaurants that serve them. Look for:

Cantonese at An Lo Yuan, 232 Tun Hua N Rd, Tel. 715-4929. Specializes in roast suckling pig.

Szechwan at Rong Shing, 45 Chin Lin Rd., 521-5340; and, Lien An, 4th Floor, 425 Tun Hua S Rd., 721-3587.

Hunan cuisine is served at Peng Yuan, 63 Nanking E Rd., Sec. 4, 541-9102.

Vegetarian, served at a number of restaurants around the city, contrary to popular belief, is anything but bland. Chinese chefs manage to make beancurd taste like chicken, beef, pork, or fish. Try Meilin Vegetarian, 3 Linsen N Rd., 391-0273; Peace Vegetarian Restaurant, 177 Hoping E Rd., Sec. 1, 3rd Floor, 341-2239; Vegetarian House, 70 Huaining St, 314-2020; Hong Lin, 36 Po Ai Rd., 2nd Floor, 361-2397.

Peking Duck, and other northern-style dishes at the Celestial Kitchen, 1 Nanking W Rd., 563-2171; Tao Jan Ting 16, Alley 4, Lane 49 Chung Hsiao E Rd., Sec. 4 781-7738; and, Genuine Peiping, located on Chung Hwa Road at the Chung Hwa Market, Block 7, 2nd Floor, 312-1001.

Kiangche at Hsiang Yuan, 6, Lane 27, Jen Ai Rd., Section 4, 771-8866.

Taiwanese at Hsing Yeh, 7, Lane 19, Shuang Cheng St., 592-5555.

Mongolian Barbecue enables customers to eat all they like for about NT$250. Thin sliced meat with a variety of vegetables and sauces barbecued on a grill. Try the Mandarin Hotel, 166 Tunhua N Rd. and, The Ploughman's Inn, 8, Lane 460, Tun Hwa S Rd., 733-3268.

Dumplings come in a variety of forms, fried, steamed and boiled and filled with beef and pork. Look for them at Tung Men Dumpling Restaurant, 37, Lane 31, Chinshan S Rd., Sec. 2, 341-1685.

FOREIGN FOOD. Of course, Taipei also has many restaurants specializing in Western cuisine. You'll find:

Swiss/German food at Zum Fass, No. 55, Basement, Lane 119, Lin Shen N Rd., 531-3815; and, Chalet Swiss, 47 Nanking E Rd., Sec. 4, 781-2051.

Italian delights at La Bettola, 57 Wen Lin Rd., Shihlin, 882-8290.

Indonesian style of cuisine at Pulau Kelapa, 738 Ting Chow St., 391-4717.

Burmese at Burma Mandalay Restaurant, 722, Ting Chow St., 351-8282.

Vietnamese at Tsui Tuan Vietnam, 20-3 Shinsheng S Rd., Sec. 3, 396-5005.

Indian dishes and delicacies at Gaylord, 328 Sung Chiang Rd., 543-4004.

Pubs, the watering holes frequented by most expatriates, dominate the Shuangcheng Street area behind the Ambassador Hotel. Dozens of pubs there offer inexpensive food, music and darts. The Ploughman Group of Pubs, conveniently located around the city are particularly popular. They include: The Ploughman, 9, Lane 25, Shuang Cheng St.; The Ploughman's Inn, 8, Lane 460, Tun Hua N Rd.; and, The Ploughman's Cottage, 305 Nanking E Rd., Sec. 3.

SEE A MOVIE in your own private viewing booth at one of the city's many MTV centers. For about NT$100 per person you'll find the latest movies and rock videos. The price includes a beverage. Just look for the neon MTV signs.

NAME CHOPS made from buffalo horn, ivory, jade, hardwood, plastic or rubber can be carved with your name in Chinese or English. Chop carving is a minor artform and some people collect chops the way others collect coins or stamps. Chopmakers have shops throughout the city, but they proliferate in Heng Yang Road near New Park. Or try Tien Shih Chi, 45 Heng Yang Rd., which is open from 9 a.m. to 9 p.m.

FAKE Rolex watches and other authentic-looking name brands are available in Snake Alley, from vendors in night markets, along the sidewalk in the Ding Hao area, and on Lin Sen North Road, near the Imperial Hotel (where there are no visible vendors, but peddlers will quietly approach you.) The imitations are good enough to impress your friends and enemies.

HANDMADE PAPER is available at the Taiwan Handicraft Paper Manufacturing Co., 47-2 Chang An W. Rd., which was first opened by the Japanese in 1935. This light, almost translucent paper is tough and durable. Cotton or *kozo* paper can be used for making clothes and *hsuan* paper for scrolls and as art paper. The company's handmade paper can also be used to make handsome cards and books. Several other paper shops are also located on this street. These stores also sell a wide variety of Chinese paper-cuttings.

CHINESE KITES can be purchased at the Rising Sun Kite Handicraft Co., Room 702, 42 Song Kiang Rd., 531-4931.

PRIVATE ART GALLERIES include Caves Gallery, 3/F, 153 Chung Hsiao E Rd., Sec. 4, 771-3769; Hsiung Shih Gallery, 9/F, 385 Tun Hwa N Rd., 772-1158; Lung Men Art Gallery, 3/F, 218 Chung Hsiao E Rd., Sec. 4, 781-6596; and, the Taipei Art Guild, the first gallery established in Taipei, 7, Lane 728, Chungshan N Rd., Sec. 6, 871-8465.

THE CULTURAL BUS, which runs on the half-hour on Sundays and national holidays from 8:30 a.m. to 5:30 p.m. is one of the best ways to see Taipei's famous sights, as well as the city and its environs. The North Route stops at the Taipei Railway Station, New Park, Chiang Kai-shek Memorial Hall, the Holiday Flower Market, the Howard Plaza Hotel, Sun Yat-sen Memorial Hall, Jung Hsin Park, the Ritz Hotel, the Martyrs Shrine,

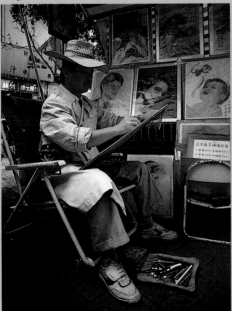

the National Palace Museum, the Chinese Culture and Movie Center, Shuanghsi Park, the Taipei Fine Arts Museum, the Fortuna Hotel, the Ambassador Hotel and then back to the Taipei Railway Station. The South Route stops at the Taipei Railway Station, the Lai Lai Sheraton Hotel, the Tinhow Shopping Center, the Fortune Dai-ichi Hotel, Sun Yat-sen Memorial hall, the Taipei World Trade Center, the Howard Plaza Hotel, the Holiday Flower Market, the Postal Museum, the National Museum of History, Youth Park, Lungshan Temple, the Armed Forces Museum, North Gate and the Taipei Railway Station. The ticket for the bus costs just NT$8 and you can get on and off anywhere along the route using just one ticket. The bus stops to pick up passengers for the comprehensive tour along the way on major streets and at many hotels throughout the city.

COMPUTERS AND PERIPHERALS are available at the Chung Hwa Market on Chung Hwa Road and at the Kwang Hwa Market at the intersection of Pateh Road and Hsinsheng South Road located under the overpass.

LIVE JAZZ is featured every Sunday afternoon at the Farmer's Pub on Shuangcheng Street.

MARBLE comes from the rugged mountain areas of eastern Taiwan. Taiwan is famous for its marble and local craftsmen make good use of the locally abundant material. Products, to name just a few, include vases, cups, plates, ashtrays, lamp stands, paper weights, bookends, bowls, chessboards, cigarette boxes and even tables and benches. Hwalien, a major source of marble in Taiwan, has marble sidewalks and the airport is constructed with marble. Try the government-run Retired Service Engineering Agency (RSEA) Display Center at 10th Fl., 207 Song Chiang Rd., 503-8225.

CHINESE ART REPRODUCTIONS, of especially good quality, are available at shops in the National Palace Museum and the National Museum of History in the downtown area.

CLOISONNE can be found in a number of stores located on Nanking East Road and in alleys off Chungshan North Road.

TRADITIONAL CHINESE-STYLE FURNITURE, including Taiwanese country-style furniture, is mainly made with wood imported from Southeast Asia, such as rosewood, ebony, sandalwood, and teak. The wood is soaked for three years, dried naturally and then baked in kilns for two months. Furniture is pieced together with wooden nails, stakes and glue — absolutely no nails are used — and then varnished at least seven to 10 times. Furniture shops are clustered on Changsha Street and Chilin Road in Taipei and on Chungshan North Road, Section 5 in Shihlin.

Members of the Paiwan ethnic group of upland Taiwan. *Taiwan's non-Han Chinese indigenous groups today number around 310,000. The Paiwan and other groups are related linguistically to the peoples of Southeast Asia.*

Land and People

Taiwan is located 160 kilometers (100 miles) off the coast of mainland China, separated from Fukien Province by the Taiwan Straits. The northern tip of the island is 1000 kilometers south of Japan and the southern tip is 350 kilometers north of the Philippines. The total area is 36,000 square kilometers and the island is 394 kilometers long and 144 kilometers wide at its widest point. South-Central Taiwan is bisected by the Tropic of Cancer. Mountains and hills cover two-thirds of the island's rugged, volcanic surface.

Taiwan has a population of 19.5 million people and is one of the most densely populated areas in the world, with 535 persons per square kilometer. In addition to the Han Chinese inhabitants of the island, there are 310,000 indigenous non-Han peoples, more than half living in mountain areas.

Taipei lies in the northern part of Taiwan and is located in an alluvial basin. The area of the city is 272 square kilometers, but only 6,698 hectares represent the original site of the city. When Taipei was made a special municipality in 1967, six satellite towns were added with an area of 20,516 hectares. The population in 1985 was 2.5 million.

How to Get There
By air:
Sixteen international airlines fly to Taiwan regularly. Chiang Kai-shek International Airport is 40 kilometers (24.8 miles) from Taipei.

By boat:
The only passenger ship serving Taiwan is the Japanese Arimura Line which sails weekly between Keelung and Okinawa and Japan. For more information contact Yung An Maritime Co., 11 Ren Ai Road, Section 3, Taipei, (02)771-5911.

Customs and Visas

All visitors to Taiwan must have a passport or travel document with a validity of more than six months and visas should be obtained before leaving for Taiwan. Visas are available at Taiwan's diplomatic, consular or representative offices abroad. Visa holders may stay in Taiwan for sixty days. This may be extended a maximum of two times by applying at the Foreign Affairs Office of the Taipei Municipal Police Administration, 89 Ninghsia Rd., 537-3680.

Each visitor may take out no more than US$1,000 or its equivalent in other foreign currencies from Taiwan unless the money was brought into the country and was declared upon arrival. If more than NT$8,000 in cash is brought into the country it must be declared upon arrival. If it is not declared it may be confiscated. No more than NT$8,000 in cash and 20 coins may be taken out of the country. If you want to reconvert New Taiwan dollars back to foreign currency upon departure, be sure to save your receipts when you change money. All persons 20 and over may bring in one bottle of wine and one carton of cigarettes duty free.

Airport Information

Inexpensive and convenient air-conditioned shuttle buses leave every 15 minutes for Taipei, stopping at several hotels, and the Sungshan Domestic Airport located right in the city. The fare is NT$72 and tickets can be purchased in the arrival terminal or outside near the boarding area. Taxis are available outside the arrivals terminal and the fare to Taipei is NT$1,000. The trip takes 45 to 60 minutes depending on the time of day. There are no porters at the airport, but baggage carts are available. There is also a Visitor's Center at the airport where hotel rooms can be reserved. A departure tax of NT$200 is collected before check-in at the airport.

Bargaining

Department stores and most large stores have set prices, but bargaining is possible at markets, streetside stalls and smaller shops.

Buses

City buses travel to all parts of Taipei, although they are sometimes very crowded. The fare is NT$7 for a regular bus and NT$8 for an air-conditioned bus. The buses are marked with a route number, but all the bus-stop signs along the way are written in Chinese. A 10-ride ticket can be purchased for NT$66 at the little newspaper kiosks along the street. For the air-conditioned buses, however, exact fare is required.

Car Rentals

Hertz Rent-A-Car has several service centers in Taipei, Taoyuan, Taichung and Kaohsiung and rentals can be returned to any service center. In Taipei call 717-3673. For Chiang Kai-shek International Airport call (03)383-3666 extension 8012. Central Auto Service, 881-9545, offers day and long-term car rentals.

Driving

An international driver's license is required. A local license may be obtained without taking the driving test if you have a valid license from your home country or an international driver's license. You will need to take a physical and an eye examination if you want to apply for a Taiwan license. If you are involved in an accident call the Foreign Affairs Police 537-3852. Driving can be a hazardous affair for those unfamiliar with Taiwan's drivers, so proceed with caution.

Communication

Telephones may be found on the street and at restaurants. Local calls are NT$1 for three minutes and long distance calls within Taiwan are NT$5. After your three minutes are up the call will automatically be cut off and you must redial. Red telephones are for local calls only. Local and long distance calls both may be made with the light blue telephones. Long distance telephone calls may also be made at any office of the International Telecommunications Administration (ITA). To place an international long distance call dial 100 for the international operator. If you are looking for the number of a person or company with an English name, call the English Speaking Directory for assistance at 311-6796.

International cables and telexes may be sent from any ITA office. Telexes may also be sent from major hotels. The main ITA office, at 28 Hangchow South Road, Section 1 (beside the Chiang Kai-shek Memorial Hall), is open 24 hours and also has facsimile service. Ring the bell if the door is closed.

Electricity
110 volts (60 cycles)

Emergencies
Dial 110 for police or 511-9564 for the Foreign Affairs Police. In case of a fire or if in need of an ambulance dial 119.

Festivals and Holidays
Many Chinese holidays are determined by the lunar calendar and so their dates vary from year to year. Therefore, only the months are given here.

January-February
Chinese New Year, the most important holiday of the year for the Chinese, falls on the first day of the first lunar month. Many restaurants and stores close for three to five days to celebrate the holiday and Taipei appears deserted with most people returning to their homes around the island to be with their families. It is very difficult to travel around the island at this time as all buses, trains and airplanes are very crowded with people returning home.

The Lantern Festival marks the end of the New Year festival. The Chinese used to believe that ghosts could be seen by the light of the first full moon and so torches were used for visibility. Nowadays lanterns are used to round off the new year festivities. In the evening children make lanterns and carry them through the streets. Large temples also display colorful lanterns on this day.

January 1
Founding Day of the Republic of China, as well as Western New Year. January 1 and 2 are national holidays in Taiwan.

March-April
The Birthday of Kuan Yin, the Goddess of Mercy is mainly celebrated at the Lungshan Temple.

March 29
Youth Day is a national holiday.

April 5
Tomb Sweeping Day is the day when Chinese families visit the burial places of relatives to tidy up the grave and make offerings.

May-June
The Birthday of Kuan Kung, the God of War is celebrated during the fifth lunar month.

The Birthday of Matsu, Goddess of the Sea, is important to the seafaring Taiwanese.

The Dragon Boat Festival — one of the most colorful festivals of the year — commemorates the death of Chu Yuan, a popular Chinese stateman and poet. The biggest dragon boat race can be seen on the Tamshui River in Taipei. Also celebrated as Poet's Day.

Also in the fifth lunar month is the Birthday of Cheng Huang, the City God of Taipei. Parades are usually held near the Cheng Huang Temple on Ti Hua Street, with stilt walking and dragon and lion dances.

August
The seventh lunar month is Ghost Month. The gates of hell are opened on the first day of the month and ghosts are allowed to return to visit their former homes. Families burn incense and paper money and place food-laden tables in front of houses and stores throughout Taipei.

September 28
Confucius' Birthday — A special ceremony is held at the Confucius Temple, using traditional costumes and ancient musical instruments.

September-October
For the Mid-Autumn (Moon) Festival, Chinese gather in parks, on mountains and at the seashore to watch the full moon, believed to be rounder and more beautiful on this day. Chinese present friends with mooncakes, moon-shaped pastries stuffed with a variety of sweets.

October 10
The National Day of the Republic of China, marking the fall of the Ching Dynasty in 1911. The day is often called the "double tens" and is celebrated with a big parade held in the morning in front of the Presidential Building on Jen Ai Road. The President usually makes a public appearance on this patriotic day.

October 25
Retrocession Day marks the return of Taiwan to the Republic of China by the Japanese in 1945. A national holiday.

October 31
Chiang Kai-shek's Birthday is a national holiday.

November 12
This is the Birthday of Sun Yat-sen, the founding father of the Republic of China. It is a national holiday in Taiwan.

December 25
Constitution Day, a national holiday.

Health and Medical Care

Travelers who have stayed in cholera-infected areas for more than five days must receive cholera immunization prior to arrival. Smallpox vaccination is no longer required.

Water must be boiled before drinking, and it is advisable to peel all fruit because of the heavy use of pesticides in Taiwan.

Taiwan has well-trained medical personnel and there are several good hospitals in Taipei, where doctors and nurses speak English. Foreigners living in Taipei use the following hospitals: Taiwan Adventist Hospital, 424 Pa Teh Road, Section 2, (771-8151); Central Clinic, 77 Chung Hsiao East Road, Section 4, (751-0221); Chang Gung Memorial Hospital, 199 Tun Hua North Road, (713-5211); Mackay Memorial Hospital, 92 Chung Shan North Road, Section 2, (543-3535); Veterans General Hospital, 201 Shi Pai Road, Section 2, (871-2121). Taiwan Adventist Hospital also has a good dental clinic.

Hotels

Expensive
The Ambassador Hotel
  63 Chung Shan North Road
  Section 2, 551-1111
Asiaworld Plaza
  100 Tun Hwa North Road, 715-0077
Brother Hotel
  255 Nanking East Road, Section 3, 712-3456
Grand Hotel
  1 Chung Shan North Road, Section 4, 596-5565
Hilton International Taipei
  38 Chung Hsiao West Road, Section 1, 311-5151
Hotel Royal Taipei
  37-1 Chungshan North Road, Section 2, 542-3266
Howard Plaza
  160 Jenai Road, Section 3, 700-2323
Imperial Hotel
  600 Lin Shen North Road, 596-3333

Lai Lai Sheraton
  12 Chung Hsiao East Road, Section 1, 321-5511
Mandarin Hotel
  166 Tun Hwa North Road, 712-1201
President Hotel
  9 Tehhwei Street, 595-1251
The Ritz Hotel
  155 Minchuan East Road, 597-1234

Moderate
Angel Hotel
  199 Sung Chiang Road, 502-9131
Century Plaza Hotel
  132 Omei Street, 311-3131
Cosmos Hotel
  43 Chung Hsiao West Road, Section 1, 361-7856
First Hotel
  63 Nanking East Road, Section 2, 541-8234
Holiday Hotel
  31 Chung Hsiao East Road, Section 1, 391-2381
Hotel China Taipei
  14 Kuan Chien Road, 331-9521
Hotel Flowers
  19 Hankow Street, Section 1, 312-3811
The Leofoo
  168 Chang Chun Road, 581-3111

Bargain
Miramar Hotel
  3 Nanking East Road, Section 2, 511-1241
Orient Hotel
  85 Hankow Street, Section 1, 331-7211
Pacific Hotel
  111 Kun Ming Street, 311-3335
Pan American Hotel
  88 Hankow Street, Section 1, 314-7305
Peace Hotel
  150 Chung Hwa Road, Section 1, 331-3161
Rainbow Guest House
  91 Chungshan North Road, Section 3, 596-5515
White House Hotel
  16 Hankow Street, Section 1, 331-7802
YMCA
  19 Hsuchang Street, 311-3201
YWCA
  7 Chingtao West Road, 371-4993

Hostels
International House
  18 Hsin Yi Road, Section 3, 707-3151
Namaste Hostel
  11-8 Fu Chou Street, 4th Fl., 393-5401
Taipei Hostel
  11, Lane 5, Lin Shen North Road, 6th Fl., 395-2951
Taipei International Youth Activity Center
  30 Hsin Hai Road, Section 3, 709-1770
Youth Hostel
  11-A Fu Chou Street, 4th Fl., 393-5401

Hours

Most government agencies are open weekdays from 8:30 a.m. to 12:00 noon and from 1:00 p.m. until 5:30 p.m. On Saturdays government offices are only open in the morning. Banks are open from 9:00 a.m. until 3:30 p.m. and from 9:00 a.m. until 12:00 or 1:00 p.m. on Saturdays.

Big department stores are generally opened from 10:00 a.m. until 10:00 p.m. daily, but check before going to make sure.

Language

Mandarin Chinese is the national dialect — as it is on the mainland — and it is taught in all the schools. The majority of the island's inhabitants originally came from Fukien and so can also speak the Fukien dialect. About 20 percent of the people speak Hakka. Most Taiwan-born people over the age of 60 attended Japanese schools during the occupation and so can speak Japanese. There are also several local dialects spoken by the island's indigenous non-Han population.

Media

Taipei has two English-language daily newspapers. The *China-Post* comes out in the morning and the *China-News* is an afternoon paper. International Community Radio Taipei (ICRT) broadcasts music, news and other programs 24 hours a day on FM 100.1 and 100.9, and AM1548. There are three local television stations which broadcast a few programs in English every week.

Money

The New Taiwan dollar is issued in coins and banknotes. Coins come in NT$1, NT$5, and NT$10 denominations. Banknotes are issued in denominations of NT$10, NT$50, NT$100, NT$500, and NT$1,000.

The Bank of Taiwan exchanges money at the Chiang Kai-shek Airport. Foreign currency can be changed at designated banks, hotels and some large department stores. American Express Card holders can cash personal checks at the American Express office, 214 Tun Hwa North Road, Taipei. Visa card holders can obtain emergency funds at the Bank of America, 205 Tun Hwa North Road, Taipei.

Museums and Memorial Halls

Armed Forces Museum, 243 Kui Yang Street, Section 1. Military displays showing the history of the armed forces of the Republic of China. Open 8:30 to 12:00, 1:00 to 4:00 p.m. Closed Tuesdays.
Butterfly Museum, 71 Chinan Road, Section 1. This private collection of thousands of local and foreign species may be seen by special arrangement by calling Prof. Chen Wei-shou, at 321-6256. Hours 9:00 a.m. to 5:00 p.m. by appointment.

Chiang Kai-shek Memorial Hall, 21 Chungshan South Road. A collection of the late President's clothes, personal belongings and photos. Open 9:00 a.m. to 5:00 p.m. daily.
The Chinese Movie and Cultural Center, 34 Chihshan Road, Section 2, Shihlin. A movie set for making traditional Chinese movies. Also houses a wax museum and a hall of Chinese costumes. Open 8:30 a.m. to 5:30 p.m.
Museum of Chinese Opera, National Fu Hsing Dramatic Arts Academy, 177 Neihu Road, Section 2. A variety of displays and video presentations on traditional Chinese opera.
National Museum of History, 49 Nanhai Road. Chinese art and archaeological artifacts. Open 9:00 a.m. to 5:00 p.m. daily.
National Palace Museum, Waishuanghsi, Shihlin. The largest and most comprehensive collection of Chinese art in the world. A must for visitors. Open 9:00 a.m. to 5:00 p.m. daily.
Postal Museum, 45 Chungking South Road, Section 2, 9:00 a.m. to 5:00 p.m. daily. Closed Mondays.
Taipei Fine Arts Museum, 181 Chungshan North Road, Section 3. Collection of modern art. Open 10:00 a.m. to 6:00 p.m. (Closed Mondays)
Taiwan Provincial Museum, located inside New Park. 9:00 a.m. to 5:00 p.m. (Closed Mondays and Wednesdays).

Police

The Foreign Affairs Police is the division of the National Police Administration which deals exclusively with foreigners. Most of the police officers in this division speak English. 537-3852, 511-9564.

Religion

The beliefs of the Chinese in Taiwan are a mixture of Buddhism, Taoism and Confucianism. There are an estimated 600,000 Catholics and Protestants, almost equally divided between the two, and about 54,000 Moslems.

Taxis

Taipei has a glut of taxis and it is never hard to find one. Few taxi drivers speak English and so it is recommended to carry directions written in Chinese. In the city passengers pay according to the meter; for longer rides outside the city agree on a price beforehand.

The current fare is NT$24 for the first kilometer and NT$6 for each additional 500 meters.

Time and Calendar

Taipei time is eight hours ahead of GMT. The official year in the Republic of China is calculated from the date of the 1911 revolution which brought China's last dynasty to an end. This follows the

traditional Chinese practice of counting years from the installment date of the emperor. To figure out the correct year either add 11 years to the Chinese date or subtract 11 years from the Western. For example, the year 1990 in Taiwan is written as the year 79, or the 79th year of the Republic of China. This is the official year and is used throughout the island.

Tipping

Generally speaking, tipping is not necessary in Taiwan. Hotels and large restaurants automatically add a 10 percent service charge to bills and so no extra tip is necessary unless special service has been given. Taxi drivers do not expect tips. NT$20 per piece of luggage is standard at air and sea ports.

Toilets

Toilets in public places and smaller restaurants and stores are usually the squat type, and so it is best to make use of restrooms in hotels and fastfood restaurants. Always bring some toilet paper along with you because many restrooms do not provide this amenity.

Tourist Information Offices

A wide variety of tourist brochures and information may be obtained at the Tourism Bureau, 9th Fl., 280 Chunghsiao East Road, Section 4, 721-8541.

The Pacific Area Travel Association also has a tourist information hot line providing travel information, emergency assistance, lost and found services and help with language problems. Call the association at (02) 717-3737.

Tours

The following reliable companies offer tours in and around Taipei, in air-conditioned buses with bilingual guides:

China Express Transportation Co., 68 Chungshan North Road, Section 2, 541-6466; Pinho Travel Service Co., 3rd Fl., 142-1 Chihlin Road, 551-4136; South East Travel Service Co., Chungshan North Road, Section 2, 571-3001; and, Taiwan Coach Tours, Rm 802, 27 Chungshan North Road, Section 3, 595-5321.

Water

Water must be boiled before drinking. Water served in hotels and restaurants is either boiled, distilled or bottled mineral water.

Weather

Taiwan has a subtropical climate with hot and humid summers and short but mild winters. The average temperature in the north is 22 centigrade and the average temperature in the south is 24.5 centigrade. The typhoon season runs from June until September.

What to Wear

Light-weight, washable clothing is recommended for most of the year, but light-weight woolens and coats are necessary for the winter.

Index

All the photos in this book were taken by
R. Ian Lloyd, except for those on pages 56 and
57 which are by *Dan Rocovitz.*